A
Shepherd's
Guide
to
Counseling
Fundamentals

Caring
for the
Flock

A
Shepherd's
Guide
to
Counseling
Fundamentals

Beth Robinson

HEARTSPRING PUBLISHING · JOPLIN, MISSOURI

Copyright © 2006
College Press Publishing Co.
Toll-free order line 800-289-3300
On the web at www.collegepress.com

Cover design by Mark A. Cole

International Standard Book Number 978-0-89900-694-9

Caring for the Flock
Series Introduction

Shepherding evokes idyllic images of green pastures, fluffy sheep, and carefree shepherds lounging in the grass. But shepherding is not all lazy days spent by a babbling brook. Shepherding involves hard work; in fact it can be downright demanding. The sheep, unfortunately, do not possess an enormous amount of intelligence, and they find themselves quite often in need of the shepherd's care and assistance. So the shepherd spends his days watching for predators, caring for injuries, searching for strays, delivering newborn lambs, and directing his flock to the right pastures.

It is in these images that God chose to communicate not only how He cares for us, but also how church leaders are to care for the church. We see in the New Testament admonitions to "be shepherds of God's flock," "be examples to the flock," and "keep watch over yourselves and all the flock." And the very word that Ephesians 4:11 labels "pastor" finds its roots in the Greek word for shepherd. God's people are led by modern-day shepherds, and while you won't see a minister extracting thorns from a member's wool or directing the Sunday school class with a staff and rod, he performs the same types of tasks. Preachers, elders, deacons, ministry leaders are frequently seen counseling a grieving widow, teaching from God's Word, or celebrating a baptism. It is through the everyday tasks of church life that leaders exercise care for their flocks.

We want to spur your growth as a shepherd. The goal of this

series is to encourage spiritual wholeness, the development of leaders, and counseling skills. As you minister to your congregation, you will face situations that stretch and challenge you, so you will find these books a concise and ready reference. It is our desire that the Caring for the Flock Series will help address the needs and concerns every shepherd faces.

This book is dedicated to *Dr. Steven Joiner*,
my boss and my mentor,
who continues to encourage me
to use my God-given talents to serve the Kingdom.

Acknowledgments

The idea of writing this book occurred as the result of teaching graduate courses to ministry students who helped me begin to organize my counseling ideas and experiences into teaching units. Eventually those teaching units became the basis for a series of books about counseling skills for ministry. I am appreciative of my graduate students who have helped me hone my ideas into a book format.

Dr. Steven Joiner, Chair of the College of Biblical Studies and Behavioral Sciences at Lubbock Christian University, gave me the first opportunity to teach a graduate ministry class. He has continued to encourage my writing and interests in working in ministry areas. He has been a wonderful boss and kind mentor in my professional development.

As I was in the early stages of developing this material, Mark Moore, a professor at Ozark Christian College and representative of College Press, contacted me to see if I had any interest in writing a manuscript for ministers that would address counseling skills. His vision of a series of books to address counseling skills for ministers spurred me to continue the work on this manuscript.

Ultimately, I have had the opportunity to work with Dru Ashwell and Jessica Scheuermann at College Press. Both of them have been encouraging, insightful, and entirely too patient with my progress on this project. My prayer is that God will continue to use them and College Press in his service.

God has blessed my life so richly with the presence of Treca, Christi, Gerrit, and Dawson. They continue to teach me about love, grace, and mercy. There are not words to express how grateful I am that they are willing to share my life. I am blessed.

Table of Contents

Introduction   11

1. On the Front Line   13

2. Stages of the Counseling Process   22

3. The Counseling Relationship   34

4. Understanding Crisis Intervention   44

5. Understanding Life Transitions   55

6. Understanding Relationship Problems   67

7. Understanding Mental Illness   76

8. What Now?   86

Glossary of Terms   90

Introduction

I've written *A Shepherd's Guide to Counseling Fundamentals* to help equip ministers to respond to the counseling needs of the members of their congregations in a godly and effective manner. While individuals frequently seek out ministers to assist with counseling issues, many ministers have limited training about counseling strategies and techniques.

The purpose of this book is to provide a brief overview of the counseling process and the different types of counseling interventions. It is intended to be an introduction to counseling for ministers rather than focusing on techniques or strategies. This book is the first in a series of books that will address pastoral care issues. The ideas presented briefly in this book will be explored in more depth in additional books in the series.

The glossary at the end of the book provides a listing of terms used in this book and additional terms that are commonly used in counseling to help the reader learn the language of counseling.

On The Front Line

Gerald entered ministry to address the spiritual concerns of his congregation. He had anticipated preaching sermons, teaching Bible classes, and having one-on-one Bible studies. He even recognized that he would minister to people in times of crisis, but he had not anticipated the number of people who would come to him seeking advice and counseling about personal issues. People came to his office with an array of issues including:

"I think my wife is having an affair."

"I was raped several months ago, and I keep having bad dreams."

"My boyfriend is hitting me."

"Since my mother died, I'm sad all the time. I can't seem to get out of bed and do anything."

"I'm hearing voices telling me that I am evil."

"I've gotten myself in a bind at work. I don't see any way out of the situation. I'm thinking about ending it all."

Frankly, Gerald felt overwhelmed by the counseling demands of his congregation and wasn't sure how many of the issues and situations he should try to help with and which ones he should send to a professionally trained counselor to handle. He firmly believed that the Bible could provide guidance and direction for all types of life situations, but he was beginning to realize that there were times when people weren't ready or just couldn't begin to process what he had to share. They needed more help than he could provide.

If you are like Gerald, you have found yourself on the front line in providing counseling services for members of your congregation and for people in your community. You may be overwhelmed, but you are recognizing that counseling is an essential, if not imperative, part of your ministry.[1] For decades, Americans have turned to ministers for help with personal problems and mental health issues. In fact, the first person that most Americans turn to for help with personal problems is a minister.[2] Actually, ministers (41%) were preferred over doctors (29%), psychiatrists and psychologists (21%), social service agencies and social workers (18%), attorneys (13%), and marriage counselors (12%).[3]

Ministers spend approximately 2.5 to 12 hours per week in counseling activities.[4] Researchers have generally found that ministers spend between ten and twenty percent of their time in counseling,[5] and they are more likely to engage in counseling activities as the size of their congregation grows larger.[6] The tendency is for ministers to counsel members of their congregation more often and to refer nonmembers to other helping professionals.[7]

While it might be expected that the majority of counseling done by ministers would focus on spiritual issues, the reality is that ministers encounter the same types of problems presented to mental health professionals.[8] People with a full range of emotional and psychological difficulties will come to visit with ministers.[9] However, ministers seem to encounter some issues more often than they do others.

Ministers report that people frequently seek their counsel in issues related to marriage and family concerns.[10] Marriage difficulties were rated as the number one or number two concern in 10 of 11 studies reviewed by Arnold & Schick.[11] In fact, religious counseling was preferred over other counseling approaches for marriage and family problems by both people who attend church frequently and those who attend church infrequently.[12]

In addition to marital and family concerns, ministers frequently encounter issues related to depression, anxiety, guilt, grief, and feelings of inadequacy.[13] They are also most often sought for crisis situations associated with grief or depression,[14] and 85% of ministers reported having counseled dangerous or suicidal persons.[15] Perhaps the most surprising information is that a person was as likely to seek counsel from a minister as a mental health professional when dealing with a serious psychiatric disorder. A minister might be asked to intervene with people dealing with major depression, bipolar disorder, panic disorders, schizophrenia, and personality disorders.[16] Quite literally, ministers are as likely as mental health professionals to have a severely mentally distressed person come to them for counseling.[17]

Despite being on the front line of counseling, ministers view their preparation in counseling as less than adequate.[18] Their training is deficient in theoretical areas of counseling, applied areas of counseling, and the application of psychological theory to actual counseling situations.[19]

For example, when providing counseling services for a variety of psychological problems, ministers usually provide spiritual strategies such as praying with the person, identifying with the person, urging a more active life, and suggesting Bible reading.[20] These strategies are obviously effective in dealing with spiritual concerns, adjustment issues, and emotional concerns. However, learning strategies from more traditional counseling approaches can give ministers additional tools to use with people struggling with emotional issues, crisis situations, and mental illness.

In addition to providing general spiritual guidance, some ministers are familiar with basic counseling strategies: reflection of feeling, reflection of content, clarification, and attending behaviors.[21] These counseling strategies are needed, but adding other skills such as conceptualization of the problem, setting goals, and knowing when and how to refer out to other better trained professionals will make their interventions more effective.

Counseling as an Aspect of Ministry

Ministry and counseling are both helping relationships. Both require a setting that permits one seeking help to make contact with someone capable of giving help.[22] Ministers may provide educational instruction, spiritual mentoring, interviewing and referral, and counseling services. Each of these types of helping relationships is different.

The purpose of *educational instruction* is to provide information to individuals who are interested in learning. Typically, ministers provide this information in the form of sermons, Bible classes, and Bible lessons. In this helping relationship, a person is seeking spiritual information and the minister is providing that information in a formal setting through sermons, Bible classes, individual Bible lessons, and even homework.

In *spiritual mentoring*, ministers typically use one-to-one or small group meetings to foster spiritual and emotional growth. In this helping relationship, people are seeking a deeper relationship with God, and the minister is providing biblical information as well as encouragement. In some cases, prayer, confession, Scripture reading, community service, and a personal relationship are used to challenge people and help them grow. The purpose is to help people deal with their own spiritual weaknesses and to help them strengthen their relationships with God.

In *interviewing*, the purpose of the relationship is to identify the source of an emotional problem or spiritual challenge and decide what course of action to take. The individual wants to know the type of resources that would be effective in dealing with a problem. Generally, the minister meets with an individual once or twice with the understanding that a referral to someone else for assistance is possible if the issue cannot be addressed through spiritual teaching or mentoring. Interviewing generally occurs in a one-to-one or family setting.

In *counseling*, the purpose of the helping relationship is to help the person deal with an emotional difficulty, a relationship issue, a crisis situation, an adjustment issue, or a mental health issue. The assumption of individuals seeking a counseling relationship is that the relationship will be ongoing and that the minister who provides the counseling is capable and qualified to help with emotional and mental issues they are facing. The counseling relationship generally occurs in a confidential office situation with only the identified client and perhaps members of the client's family present. It is important to note that there is an assumption of confidentiality in the counseling relationship.

Distinguishing Counseling from Other Relationships

Counseling is a unique professional relationship that is distinguished from other professional and personal relationships. In most personal and professional relationships, people in the relationship assume reciprocity, meaning that someone will meet some of their needs and will require some sharing of personal experiences and personal history. In contrast, counseling is based on the following concepts:

★ The needs of the client take precedence over the needs of the counselor.

★ The relationship is maintained only as long as it is necessary to assist the client.

★ The counselor will identify and address issues not broached in other relationships.

★ Confidentiality is assumed. (However, it should be noted that most individuals expect confidentiality in all their communications with ministers unless they give explicit consent to breach their confidentiality.)

It is important to distinguish counseling relationships from other relationships to prevent ministers from making mistakes as they are learning counseling skills. Violating the boundaries of a counseling relationship by pursuing a friendship, a romantic relationship, or a business relationship may be confusing to the client and may prevent therapeutic progress.

On the other hand, utilizing counseling techniques in other types of relationships may not be appreciated by friends, colleagues, and church members. Counseling techniques are directed toward creating change. Friends, colleagues, and church members may just want to be shown support or concern.

Understanding Counseling Terms

While you are primarily a minister, when you begin a counseling relationship with a church member or another individual, you are changing professional roles. Although you may have no desire to become a professional counselor, you still need to have an understanding of some of the professional terms used in a counseling relationship. Some of these terms will be used in this book. Common counseling terms include:

1. *Client:* The individual seeking help from a minister with emotional difficulties, relationship issues, crisis situations, adjustment issues, and mental health issues. A client comes to a minister specifically seeking help with an identified "problem" with the expectation that the minister has the professional skills to provide assistance.

2. *Therapeutic progress:* Progress in a counseling relationship occurs when clients become better at helping themselves and at recognizing opportunities and ways to more effectively utilize their God-given talents and abilities in the service of God's kingdom.

3. *Conceptualization:* To interpret what the client reports and what a minister observes to develop a concept of what issues are creating dysfunction in the individual's life.

A Word of Caution

As you read this book, you may begin to realize that you do not have the personal characteristics or training to provide effective counseling interventions in your role as a minister. If you have not been blessed with the talents needed to be effective in a counseling role, then use the talents God has blessed you with to serve him in other ways. However, if you believe that you have the talents to be an effective counselor, but need more training, then I would encourage you to pursue more training. Keep in mind that developing counseling relationships can be time-consuming and personally draining. When you are talking with clients about problems and challenges, it can become discouraging and disheartening. Remember: God and his guiding biblical principles ultimately change lives, not you.

Purpose of this Book

The purpose of this book is to equip ministers with the techniques and skills they need to be more effective in counseling relationships. This book will primarily focus on the development of skills to help ministers assess and intervene in situations that involve emotional difficulties, relationship issues, crisis situations, adjustment issues, and mental health issues. These tools are in no way intended to supersede the value of the spiritual tools ministers already possess. These counseling techniques are presented as a way to intervene in emotional and relationship issues that may involve elements typically addressed by mental health practitioners.

Chapter One References

[1] R.A. Bell, R.R. Morris, C.E. Holzer, & G.J. Warheit, "The Clergy as a Mental Health Resource: Parts I and II," *The Journal of Pastoral Care* 30 (1976) 103-115; M.G. Gilbert, "The Decision of Assemblies of God Pastors to Counsel or Refer," *Journal of Psychology and Theology* 9 (1981) 250-256; R.J. Givens, "The Counseling Ministry of the Churches of Christ," *Journal of Psychology and Theology* 4 (1976) 300-303; D.W. Lowe, "Counseling Activities and Referral Practices of Ministers," *Journal of Psychology and Christianity* 5 (1986) 22-29; W.M. Ziegler & G.A. Goreham, "Formal Pastoral Counseling in Rural Northern Plains Churches," *The Journal of Pastoral Care* 50 (1996) 393-404.

[2] H.P. Chalfant, P.L. Heller, A. Roberts, D. Briones, S. Aguirre-Hochbaum, & W. Farr, "The Clergy as a Resource for Those Encountering Psychological Distress," *Review of Religious Research* 31 (1990) 305-313; G. Gurin, J. Veroff, & B. Feld, *Americans View Their Mental Health* (New York: Basic Books, 1960); J. Veroff, R.A. Kulka, & E. Douvan, *Mental Health in America: Patterns of Helpseeking from 1957 to 1976* (New York: Basic Books, 1981).

[3] Chalfant et al., "Clergy as a Resource," 305-313.

[4] Ziegler & Goreham, "Formal Pastoral Counseling," 393-404.

[5] A.J. Weaver, "Has There Been a Failure to Prepare and Support Parish-based Clergy in Their Role as Frontline Community Mental Health Workers? A Review," *The Journal of Pastoral Care* 49 (1995) 129-147.

[6] G.K. Lau & R. Steele, "An Empirical Study of the Pastoral Mental Health Involvement Model," *Journal of Psychology and Theology* 18 (1990) 261-269.

[7] Ibid., 261-269.

[8] G. Domino, "Clergy's Knowledge of Psychopathology," *Journal of Psychology and Theology* 18 (1990) 32-39.

[9] E.L. Worthington, "Religious Counseling: A Review of Published Empirical Research," *Journal of Counseling and Development* 64 (1986) 421-431.

[10] A.J. Weaver, H.G. Koenig, & D.B. Larson, "Marriage and Family Therapists and the Clergy: A Need for Clinical Collaboration, Training, and Research," *Journal of Marital and Family Therapy* 23 (1997) 13-25.

[11] J.D. Arnold & C. Schick, "Counseling by Clergy: A Review of Empirical Research," *Journal of Pastoral Counseling* 14 (1979) 76-101.

[12] G. Privette, S. Quackenbos, & C.M. Bundrick, "Preferences for Religious or Nonreligious Counseling and Psychotherapy," *Psychological Reports* 75 (1994) 539-546.

[13] L.W. Abramczyk, "The Counseling Function of Pastors: A Study in Practice and Preparation," *Journal of Psychology and Theology* 9 (1981) 257-265; Bell, et al., "Clergy as Mental Health Resource," 103-115; Lowe, "Counseling Activities," 22 29; H.A. Virkler, "Counseling Demands, Procedures, and Preparation of Parish Ministers: A Descriptive Study," *Journal of Psychology and Theology* 7 (1979) 271-280; D. Winger & B. Hunsberger, "Clergy Counseling Practices, Christian Orthodoxy and Problem Solving Styles," *Journal of Psychology and Theology* 16 (1988) 41-48.

[14] R.W. Fairchild, *Finding Hope Again: A Pastor's Guide to Counseling Depressed Persons* (New York: Harper and Row, 1980).

[15] R.F. Mollica, F.J. Streets, J. Boscarino, & F.C. Redlich, "A Community Study of Formal Pastoral Counseling Activities of the Clergy," *American Journal of Psychiatry* 143 (1986) 323-328.

[16] D.B. Larson, A.A. Hohmann, L.G. Kessler, K.G. Meador, J.H. Boyd, & E. McSherry, "The Couch and the Cloth: The Need for Linkage," *Hospital and Community Psychiatry* 39 (1988) 1064-1069.

[17] A.A. Hohmann & D.B. Larson, "Psychiatric Factors Predicting Use of Clergy," in *Psychotherapy and Religious Values*, ed. by E.L. Worthington, Jr. (Grand Rapids: Baker Book House, 1993) 71-84.

[18] Arnold & Schick, "Counseling by Clergy," 76-101; D.K. Orthner, *Pastoral Counseling: Caring and Caregivers in the United Methodist*

Church (Nashville: The General Board of Higher Education and Ministry of the United Methodist Church, 1986); Virkler, "Counseling Demands," 271-280.

[19] Virkler, "Counseling Demands," 271-280.

[20] Bell, et al., "Clergy as Mental Health Resource," 103-115; Virkler, "Counseling Demands," 271-280.

[21] Abramczyk, "Counseling Function of Pastors," 257-265.

[22] L.S. Cormier & H. Hackney, *The Professional Counselor: A Process Guide to Helping* (Boston: Allyn and Bacon, 1993) 13.

Stages of the Counseling Process

When Dorothy entered Gerald's office, her eyes were red and puffy. It was obvious that she had been crying. She told Gerald that her son had gone to the army recruiting office and signed up to serve in the military. She voiced her frustrations about her son making the decision without discussing it with her. As a single parent, she felt betrayed by his lack of communication concerning such a large decision. She also discussed her fears about her son's safety with current military involvement overseas. During the conversation she cried frequently. Gerald listened and tried to reassure her about her son's safety. When Dorothy left the office, she was still crying and seemed more upset than when she came to see Gerald. After Dorothy left, Gerald sat at his desk feeling like he had done little to help Dorothy and wondering what else he could have done.

Gerald would benefit from understanding that the counseling process itself moves through stages. While providing help is the purpose of counseling and the reason why a person will come to see a minister, he must understand the stages of the counseling relationship. With an understanding of the stages of counseling, Gerald would know what to look for during the first meeting with Dorothy, and his expectations would be more realistic. The stages of the counseling process include assessment, goal setting, intervention, and evaluation of the intervention.[1]

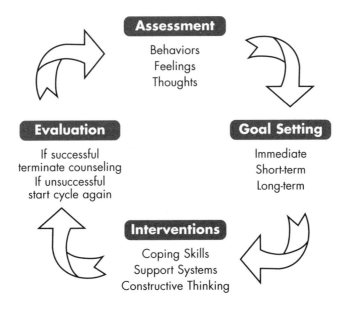

Figure 2.1 Stages of the Counseling Process

Assessment

Assessment involves observation and collecting information during the initial stages of the counseling process. Although clients continue to disclose information throughout the counseling relationship, it is during the initial stages of counseling when most disclosure occurs. Assessment permeates all counseling sessions and allows you to determine how severe the problem is, the client's current emotional status, the alternatives available, and whether the client is a danger to himself, herself, or others.

Assessment must focus on behaviors, feelings, and thoughts. Abnormal or impaired emotions are often the first indication of significant problems, especially if they involve withdrawal or overreaction. Some people will shut down emotionally when presented with an overwhelming or perplexing situation, while others will become overly emotional when faced with a difficult situation. Negative reactions may be expressed through anger, hostility, anxiety, fear, or sadness. The following questionnaire should help you during assessment to pay attention to the thought patterns, behaviors, and emotional reactions and warn you of any potential dangers. You may use the questionnaire during the counseling session and take notes about each of the questions to help you remember what the client said after the session is over. You may want to reference the questionnaire as the counseling relationship progresses to assess progress and to help you think about the challenges the client is facing. While it may be tempting to give the questionnaire to a client to fill out, it is much more effective to ask these questions in a face-to-face setting to assess nonverbal communication. In addition, some of the questions are not appropriate for clients to answer themselves. For example, would a client recognize and acknowledge that she had poor judgment? The questions do not have to be answered in a specific order. In fact a question about whether the client exhibits good judgment might be delayed until the end of the session because you will be making that determination, not the client.

Assessment Questionnaire[2]

1. How long has the problem existed?
2. How has the client tried to resolve the problem?
3. Why is the client seeking help now?
4. Does the client exhibit good judgment?
5. Is the client's hygiene and appearance appropriate?
6. Is the client's level of activity normal? Is he or she moving slowly or fidgeting a lot?
7. Do the client's emotional responses indicate that the client is denying the situation or trying to avoid it?
8. Is the client's emotional reaction influenced by other people? If so, how?
9. Do people typically show similar emotional reactions in this type of situation?
10. Is the client using drugs or alcohol to cope with the situation?
11. What type of family support does the client have?
12. Does the client have close friends that can assist with the current situation?

13. Are the client's behavioral reactions normal for the current situation or problem?

14. How would other people typically behave in this type of situation?

15. Do the client's perceptions match the reality of the situation?

16. Is the client blaming himself or others when blame isn't warranted?

17. Is the client in any current danger? If so, what?

18. Does the client present a threat to himself or others?

19. What are the client's strengths that can be utilized to address the current situation?

Recognizing Levels of Impairment

Part of the assessment process is recognizing whether clients are impaired in their emotional, behavioral, and cognitive functioning. Impairment involves the reduction of a person's ability to cope and perform daily tasks. Recognizing the level of impairment will help you determine if you have the ability to assist people who want you to help them. Without a broad range of experience, you may have difficulty recognizing levels of impairment in those seeking your counsel. While severe impairment levels are typically easy to identify, you might not recognize the more minor impairments. The following tables will aid your recognition levels. These three tables outline emotional, behavioral, and thinking impairments. When clients are experiencing moderate, marked, or severe impairment, they most likely need to be referred to a professional counselor.

Level of Impairment	Description
No Impairment	Stable mood with appropriate emotional expression
Minimal Impairment	Emotions under client's control with emotions appropriate to situation with the exception of brief periods when negative mood is expressed more intensely than a situation warrants.
Low Impairment	Client perceives emotions as being substantially under control, but there are increasingly longer periods of time when the negative mood expressed is more intense than a situation warrants.

Moderate Impairment	Client must make an effort to keep emotional control. Emotions may be inappropriate for situations and may fluctuate noticeably. Mood experienced is noticeably more intense than situation warrants.
Marked Impairment	Client does not perceive emotions as being under control. Negative emotions are experienced at a markedly higher level than the situation warrants. Emotions may be obviously inappropriate for the situation.
Severe Impairment	Emotionally erratic or having no emotional control

Table 2.1 Emotional Reaction Scale[3]

Level of Impairment	Description
No Impairment	Client performs tasks necessary for daily functioning. Coping strategies are appropriate for crisis situations.
Minimal Impairment	Client exerts considerable effort to perform tasks necessary for daily functioning. Occasional use of ineffective coping strategies when faced with crisis situations.
Low Impairment	Client neglects some tasks necessary for daily functioning and performs others with decreasing effectiveness. Occasional use of ineffective coping strategies for crisis situations.
Moderate Impairment	The client's ability to perform daily tasks is noticeably compromised. Client displays coping strategies that are ineffective and maladaptive.
Marked Impairment	Client's ability to perform daily tasks is noticeably impaired. Client displays coping skills that are likely to exacerbate the crisis situation.
Severe Impairment	Behavior is erratic and unpredictable. The client's behaviors are harmful to self or others.

Table 2.2 Behavioral Reaction Scale[4]

Level of Impairment	Description
No Impairment	Client displays normal concentration, problem-solving, and decision-making abilities. Client's perceptions and interpretation of situations match reality.
Minimal Impairment	Client's thoughts may drift, but problem-solving and decision-making skills are hardly affected. Client's perceptions and interpretation of situations generally match reality.

Low Impairment	Client perceives diminishing control of thoughts and has occasional disturbances of concentration. Client has recurrent difficulties with problem-solving and decision-making. Client's perceptions and interpretations of situations may differ from reality.
Moderate Impairment	Problem-solving and decision-making skills adversely affected by self-doubt and confusions. Frequent disturbances of concentration. Client's perceptions and interpretations of situations differ noticeably with reality.
Marked Impairment	The appropriateness of problem-solving and decision-making skills adversely affected by self-doubt and confusion. Concentration affected by intrusive thoughts. Client's perceptions and interpretation of situations may differ substantially from reality.
Severe Impairment	Inability to concentrate on anything. Problem-solving and decision-making have completely shut down. Client's perceptions and interpretations of situations differ so substantially from reality that it creates a threat to a client's welfare.

Table 2.3 Thinking Reaction Scale[5]

Setting Goals

After a preliminary assessment of the client's challenges and coping skills, you are ready to set goals. *Goal setting* sets the direction of the counseling sessions. Goals may be directed toward changing how clients act, think, feel, or relate to others. There are three types of counseling goals, ranging from immediate to long-term.

- *Immediate goals* address the imminent crisis or problems that must be addressed quickly for the emotional and physical safety of the client. Generally, these goals must be addressed during the session or within 24 hours.
- *Short-term goals* address changes in the client's behavior, thinking, or emotion. Short-term goals should be achieved within six to eight sessions.
- *Long-term goals* address deeply rooted personality issues and relationship dysfunction. Long-term goals may take from several months to several years to address depending on the client's level of functioning. When clients have significant

impairment and require that you work with them weekly to achieve long-term goals, they probably need to be referred to a professional counselor.

These goals are generally addressed in the order presented above. When possible, the goals need to be developed collaboratively with clients. When clients have input concerning goals, they are more committed to achieving goals. They are the framework for the plan of intervention. You have to deal with the immediate crisis first, then the short-term goals, and then the long-term goals. Keep in mind the clients frequently terminate counseling before you think they have satisfactorily addressed the problems. Because you never know when a client will drop out of counseling, you need to address the most urgent problems first, then address the behaviors, thoughts, and emotions that you are most likely to impact immediately. Recognize that the counseling process is cyclical (as seen in Figure 2.1), and that new immediate or short-term goals may emerge as treatment progresses.

Clients will not be able to address the deeply rooted personality and relationship issues until they are able to cope with the daily crisis and manage the stress in their lives. Ideally, every client will continue counseling until long-term goals are accomplished. However, deeply rooted issues are often difficult, and change is frequently easier to talk about than to enact. Clients may need to take incremental steps toward meeting long-term goals. Dropping out of counseling may actually be helpful if the clients use the time to stabilize their functioning so they can return with a fresh look at other more significant issues. Ideally clients will return ready to tackle more difficult issues head on and win the battle for their emotional health. On the other hand, other individuals may drop out of counseling because they do not want to address the issues targeted by long-term goals. In some cases, addressing deeply rooted personality and relationship issues can be a lifelong endeavor for clients.

Applying What You Know

Jasmine's Story

Jasmine is twenty years old and was in an automobile accident nine months ago that has left her paralyzed from the waist down. Jasmine's car was hit by a drunk driver who ran a stop sign. Jasmine's best friend, Alexis, was a passenger in the car Jasmine was driving, and she was killed in the accident. When Jasmine comes to see you, she is depressed and blames herself for the accident. She tells you, "I don't see any reason for living. I've destroyed my life and I killed Alexis. God will never forgive me for what I have done."

1. List two immediate goals:

   _____

   _____

2. List two short-term goals:

   _____

   _____

3. List two long-term goals:

   _____

   _____

There are several possible ways to word and develop the goals for Jasmine. Some possible goals include:

1. Immediate goals:
   - Address Jasmine's suicidal thoughts and intentions
   - Help Jasmine recognize that the accident was not her fault
2. Short term goals:
   - Decrease symptoms of depression
   - Develop coping strategies for anxiety and self-blaming

3. Long-term goals:
   - Identify meaningful opportunities for Jasmine to explore in regard to relationships and career decisions
   - Incorporate paralysis into a healthy identity for Jasmine and address her concerns about her relationship with God

Anthony's Story

Anthony is 33 years old and has worked in the family business since he was sixteen years old. He has completed his bachelor's degree and master's degree in business by going to school at night while continuing to work full-time with his father in the family business. Recently Anthony and his father have begun to argue about decisions related to the business. Anthony believes that his father doesn't trust him and won't listen to his ideas. As a result of the disagreements about the family business, Anthony will not attend family gatherings because he doesn't want to interact with his father during his leisure time. He won't even come to church when his father is in town because he believes his father is a hypocrite and the church is supporting his father. Anthony comes to you because he wants to start a new company that will directly compete with his father's company.

1. List two immediate goals:

   _____

   _____

2. List two short-term goals:

   _____

   _____

3. List two long-term goals:

   _____

   _____

There are several possible ways to word and develop the goals for Anthony. Some possible goals include:

1. Immediate goals:
   - Identify which issues at work are the source of the disagreements
   - Help Anthony recognize that isolating himself from his family and church is punishing him, not his father
2. Short-term goals:
   - Mediate the disagreements between Anthony and his father (if his father is willing)
   - Determine if leaving the family business is in Anthony's best interests
   - Develop strategies for dealing with stress and frustration
3. Long-term goals:
   - Strengthen Anthony's personal identity so he is not easily angered or frustrated by the actions of others
   - Develop a strategy for career development that incorporates spiritual values

If you have felt overwhelmed by the development of some of the goals in these exercises or have found that your goals are significantly different from the suggested goals, you are developing an awareness that you need additional training to provide effective counseling interventions. Clients who need to address significant long-term goals generally should be referred to a professionally trained counselor.

Interventions

Once you have assessed the client and developed some goals for counseling, the next step in the counseling process is to provide an intervention that moves the client toward the goals for the counseling relationship. The term *intervention* refers to involving yourself as a counselor in the situation to initiate growth or change in the life of the client. Developing the ability to effectively intervene is an ongoing process for all counselors. Our skills improve with experience and training. When you are working with clients who need advanced interventions, you may prefer to refer them to a professional counselor. Presenting specific interventions skills is beyond the scope of this introductory book. However, it is important that you have a general understanding of the counseling process and how it works, including the intervention phase.

Interventions focus on coping skills, support systems, and constructive thinking.

- *Coping skills* are the behaviors of the client that help the client deal with the current situation.
- *Support systems* include people in the client's life, in the present or the past, who are concerned about the client and care what happens in the client's life.
- *Constructive thinking* helps the client to consider positive ways to change their reactions to stressors.

Interventions are usually tailored to the individual needs of the client and are developed from the initial assessment. There are literally countless intervention strategies available for various counseling problems and challenges. Intervention strategies for specific issues and situations will be provided in more detail as particular counseling strategies are discussed.

Evaluation

You must evaluate the effectiveness of the intervention and be able to change it if it is not achieving its goals. To do this, several different types of information may be necessary. Not all counseling situations will require multiple ways to evaluate the effectiveness of interventions, but the following list will give you some ideas of ways to assess the effectiveness of counseling.

- Ask the client if the intervention is working
- Assess whether you believe the intervention is working
- Ask other people important to the client if they have seen any positive changes

- Use standardized assessments in some situations to assess how effective your intervention has been
- Ask the client to keep a diary of specific behaviors, thoughts, or feelings
- Recognize the ability of the client to adapt to or function in several situations such as family, school, work, etc.

If the intervention has not been successful, then restart the cycle of the counseling process as shown in Figure 2.1. A successful intervention may mean that the counseling relationship can be terminated, or another counseling issue can be addressed by following the same guidelines.

Wrapping It Up

Understanding the stages of the counseling relationship will allow you to recognize what skills and tasks are appropriate when you meet with individuals. Knowing how to assess the situation and develop goals for counseling will enable you to provide more effective interventions. When you provide interventions and you evaluate their effectiveness, it will improve your counseling skills and help you learn how to better address situations with clients in the future. Knowing the stages of the counseling relationship is not a panacea for all counseling situations, but it does provide a framework for you to more effectively provide counseling for your congregation.

Chapter Two References

[1] R.E. Dimond, R.A. Havens, & A.C. Jones, "A Conceptual Framework for the Practice of Prescriptive Eclecticism in Psychotherapy," *American Psychologist* 33 (1978) 239-248.

[2] R.K. James & B.E. Gilliland, *Crisis Intervention Strategies,* 5th ed. (Belmont, CA: Thomson Brooks/Cole, 2005) 21-31.

[3] R.A. Myer, R.C. Williams, A.J. Ottens, and E.E. Schmidt, unpublished manuscript (DeKalb, IL: Northern Illinois University, 1991).

[4] Ibid.

[5] Ibid.

The Counseling Relationship

Damon and his wife Anna frequently socialized with Gerald and his wife. They had similar interests and enjoyed visiting during church functions. Damon, a thirty-five-year-old attorney, had a successful private practice that easily supported his wife and three children. When Damon stopped Gerald after church and asked if he could meet Gerald for lunch some time during the next week, Gerald readily agreed. When they met in a local cafe for lunch, Damon asked for a secluded table in the restaurant. As Gerald waited for Damon to begin, Damon looked down at his plate and then looked away for a moment.

"I can't believe things have gotten so out of control. When it started, it was no big deal," Damon paused for a minute.

Gerald nodded, not knowing quite what to expect.

"It started when I was in junior high school. A bunch of us kids found a magazine with pictures in it. We were curious and passed it around. I saw it several times. Then it seemed like anytime I wanted to see more pictures, my friends had access to magazines their brothers or dads had. By the time I was in high school, I was accessing websites that had all kinds of pictures and showed lots of other stuff."

Gerald was surprised by the revelation, but nodded for Damon to continue.

"When I married Anna, I hid my pornography use. I used the computer at the office and kept my computer at home in our spare bedroom. It worked until last week when Anna walked in while I was at the computer. She told me I had to get help or she was going to leave me. I didn't know where else to turn. I need you to talk to Anna and convince her to stay with me." Damon's disclosure stunned Gerald. He didn't know what to do to help Damon. He was not sure if he could help Damon or not. He was a close friend to both Damon and Anna. He felt as if he might know too much about them to be objective in a counseling relationship.

Like Gerald, when you enter into a counseling relationship, you are entering into a professional alliance where you are assuming a different role than you have assumed in any other relationship. You may be quite effective in educational ministries, public speaking, and even spiritual mentoring, yet you struggle with the parameters of a counseling relationship in your ministry. The skills and techniques that have served you well in your other roles may not be as effective when you enter into a counseling relationship. Counseling is not a mentoring relationship that requires advice giving. Instead, it is designed to provide unconditional acceptance of the client. This is one of the core factors of effective counseling.

The counseling relationship is designed to help clients change their thinking and actions so they can lead more effective and meaningful lives in accordance with spiritual principles. It is a focused, goal-oriented relationship. If it is effective, clients will become better at helping themselves. They will also recognize better ways and means to utilize their God-given talents and abilities in the service of his kingdom.

The counseling relationship itself is core to therapeutic progress for clients. While it is important to understand counseling techniques and strategies, the most important tool in the counseling relationship is the minister. Successful treatment of clients has more to do with the personal characteristics of the minister than the type of treatment strategies utilized.[1] Imagine the counseling relationship as a series of building blocks (Figure 3.1):

- The personal qualities of the minister are the foundation of the counseling relationship.
- The second building block of the counseling relationship is the interpersonal skills of the minister.

- The third building block of the counseling relationship is the conceptualization skills of the minister.
- The fourth and final building block of the counseling relationship is the intervention skills of the minister.

Figure 3.1 Building Blocks of a Counseling Relationship

The Minister's Personal Qualities

There are ten personal qualities that help create effective counseling interactions. The ten personal qualities include:[2]

1. *Good will* involves your having a sincere interest in the welfare of others. You cannot be motivated by a need to be needed by others or by a need to rescue others. You cannot be motivated to meet any of your emotional needs through the counseling relationship.

2. *Emotional presence* is the ability to be present and in the moment for others. Ministers have to have the ability and willingness to be with clients in their experiences of joy and pain no matter how difficult it is to be emotionally present while clients examine and explore their emotions.

3. *Personal power* includes the recognition and acceptance of one's personal power. For ministers this means recognizing one's own strength and vitality without a need to diminish others or feel superior to them. Ministers need a particular awareness of this because clients often defer their opinions in

deference to a minister with the assumption that a minister would know more than they would.

4. *Personal counseling style* refers to finding your own counseling style. Your counseling style becomes an extension and expression of your own personality and your own God-given talents.

5. *Vulnerability* is a minister's willingness to be vulnerable and transparent in establishing relationships.

6. *Self-worth* involves recognizing and appreciating the gifts God has blessed you with. Ministers have a healthy respect for how God has manifested himself in their lives.

7. *Modeling* involves a willingness to serve as a model for your clients. You recognize the powerful influence of example as others show proper emotional and interpersonal skills. A part of this recognition includes knowing when you are exhibiting healthy versus unhealthy behaviors.

8. *Risk taking* includes your willingness to risk making mistakes and to admit having made them. In counseling and in life, we all learn from our mistakes and have to be willing to fail in order to learn.

9. *A growth orientation* involves a commitment to investing in yourself and others to change and molding yourself to become more reflective of Christ in your life. A growth orientation includes an appreciation for the gift of the time God has given us in this life and a willingness to try to use every moment to impact his kingdom.

10. *A sense of humor* allows you to enjoy life and to enjoy the challenges that develop along the way. A sense of humor allows you to show your clients the importance of not taking yourself or life's problems too seriously. Even in the most trying situations, there are frequently moments of humor.

The following exercise provides you with the opportunity to reflect on your personal qualities and how they will impact your counseling relationships. Use the following scale to answer the questions:

1=Strongly Agree   2=Agree   3=Disagree   4=Strongly Disagree

The Emotional IQ Test

_____ 1. I do not get angry when verbally attacked.

_____ 2. I am comfortable with other people's grief, even those close to me.

_____ 3. I am able to decide to love a person and then do so.

_____ 4. When I am at a social event, I am comfortable striking up conversations with strangers.

_____ 5. When I am trying to make a decision on an important issue, I try to consider both sides of the issue before deciding what to do.

_____ 6. I am comfortable with other people's anger and hate.

_____ 7. My friends know how I am feeling most of the time.

_____ 8. When I feel pressure at work, I respond by working more effectively.

_____ 9. I worry regularly in some circumstances.

_____ 10. At certain times and in some circumstances, I feel shame.

_____ 11. My anger keeps coming back in certain situations or with specific people.

_____ 12. I generally have a clear sense of purpose in my life.

_____ 13. For some things I have done in the past, I feel guilty.

_____ 14. At times I feel degraded and humiliated.

_____ 15. I frequently get anxious about certain situations.

_____ 16. I regularly feel sad about specific issues in my life.

_____ 17. I sometimes get jealous.

_____ 18. I feel stress never ends in my life.

_____ 19. I am comfortable hugging other adults.

_____ 20. I am comfortable with crying when I am sad.

_____ 21. I am comfortable saying "I love you" to the important people in my life.

_____ 22. When I get upset, I am able to express my frustration or anger without letting my emotions get out of control.

_____ 23. If I am arguing about an issue and I believe I am correct, I will agree to disagree and end the argument.

Interpersonal Skills

Personal qualities in counseling form the foundational building blocks of each successful session, but interpersonal skills are a necessity for effective results. Ministers who possess the following interpersonal skills will be able to effectively relate to others:[3]

1. *Pragmatism* is a practical and matter-of-fact way of approaching counseling situations and of solving client problems. Your emphasis is on practical applications and consequences.

2. *Competence* requires the development of the skills and knowledge to provide effective counseling interventions that will help clients learn to function more effectively and to utilize their talents and abilities in God's kingdom.

3. *Respect* for clients entails a feeling of appreciation for the uniqueness of each client. In addition, respect for clients is demonstrated through allowing clients to express opinions and reactions that may not be similar to your own.

4. *Genuineness* requires honesty and sincerity in the counseling relationship. You must honestly feel and express emotions toward the client and his or her life situations.

5. *Promotion of client self-responsibility* involves a commitment to helping clients trust God during the most stressful moments in their lives and become more self-reliant in problem solving. Clients cannot become independent and responsible if the minister allows them to rely on him for advice and guidance in solving problems.

6. *Listening* involves hearing what the client is saying. This requires you to suspend preconceptions about clients and pay close attention to verbal and nonverbal communication so that they can present an accurate picture of who they really are. Otherwise, your impressions of the clients and their situations will distort reality and delay any effective outcomes.

7. *Accurate communication* refers to the ability to understand the communication of the client. To do this, you will clarify and restate what you hear clients saying to check for accuracy. You must assess whether the client understands your communication

as well. Check back with the client to determine if he or she understands what you are saying.

8. *Trustworthiness* is the trait of deserving trust and confidence by being reliable in the eyes of the client. This means clients can depend on your being nonjudgmental in your responses. In addition, being trustworthy requires that ministers also keep the confidences that clients share with them.

Assessing Interpersonal Skills

Please put an "X" on the lines following each of the interpersonal skills to indicate how well you perceive you have mastered these skills.

1. *Pragmatism*   Poor_____Excellent

2. *Competence*   Poor_____Excellent

3. *Respect*   Poor_____Excellent

4. *Genuineness*   Poor_____Excellent

5. *Client self-responsibility* Poor_____Excellent

6. *Listening*   Poor_____Excellent

7. *Accurate communication* Poor_____Excellent

8. *Trustworthiness*   Poor_____Excellent

Conceptualization Skills

As the counseling relationship develops, a minister must have the ability to conceptualize the problem or challenge the client is facing. Conceptualization requires you to interpret what the client reports, analyze what you know about the situation or similar situations, and decide how to effectively intervene. When you become involved in the world of the client, you must be able to maintain a connection without losing perspective of the client's issues and problems. You can increase your effectiveness when you use the following skills to conceptualize the challenges facing the client:

1. You have to be able to *comprehend* what the client is trying to communicate about his or her concerns and situation and be able to place this in the context of the client's life story.
2. You must be able to *relate to the client's concerns* without becoming so immersed in the client's situation that you lose perspective or that you begin to respond based on your personal needs or concerns.
3. Once you have an awareness of the client's concerns, you need to *think through* the situation and challenges facing the client and develop a realistic understanding of the consequences and constraints of the situation.
4. As you analyze the client's situation, you begin to *recognize connections and contradictions* in his or her communications and situations.
5. Conceptualizing the client's situation and challenges ultimately requires that you be able to *understand what the connections and contradictions* mean.[4] Only when you can assign meaning to the connections and contradictions in the client's situation, can you successfully intervene.

Intervention Skills

Once you are able to conceptualize the client's problem and other counseling issues, you must develop a plan that will help the client manage the crisis or challenge in his own life.[5] For this plan to be effective, it must address the client's feelings and attitudes, thinking, behaviors, ability to change, interpersonal relationships, and interpretation of life situations. Intervention strategies can be used one time or repeatedly and may be utilized in short-term counseling relationships or long-term counseling relationships.

Interventions emerge from the conceptualization of counseling issues. Understanding the basic categories for conceptualizing issues is a prerequisite for developing intervention strategies. Too often, inexperienced counselors try to utilize intervention skills without conceptualizing the issues of the counseling situation. The rest of this book is designed to introduce you to some basic understandings of counseling issues that will provide a framework to conceptualize counseling issues.

The most foundational component of understanding counseling issues is to identify the different types of situations requiring counseling. In simple terms, counseling can be divided into the following categories: crisis intervention, life transitions, relationship problems, and mental illness. Crisis intervention refers to situations where the counseling intervention immediately follows a traumatic experience and may only last one or two sessions. Life transitions are all the changes that individuals make in their lives in regard to aging, changing family status, and career changes. Relationship problems include marital issues, parenting issues, sibling issues, friendship issues, and dating issues. Mental illness refers to issues related to significant impairment in daily functioning that may be caused by psychological, biological, environment, or spiritual issues.

Wrapping It Up

My assumption in writing this book is that you already possess the personal qualities that are required for effective ministry and counseling. In fact, I am assuming that you will already have most of the interpersonal skills required for building counseling relationships. The emphasis of this book will be for you to develop conceptualization skills to identify client issues and problems. Other books in this series will help you improve your intervention skills you need to provide effective counseling. Remember, as you grow in training and experience, your ability to conceptualize client problems and issues and to provide effective interventions will improve.

Chapter Three References

[1] L. Luborsky, et al., "The Nonspecific Hypothesis of Therapeutic Effectiveness: A Current Assessment," *American Journal of Orthopsychiatry* 56 (1986) 501-512.

[2] G. Corey, M.S. Corey, & P. Callanan, *Issues and Ethics in the Helping Professions*, 3rd ed. (Pacific Grove, CA: Brooks/Cole, 1988) 28-30.

[3] Gerard Egan, *The Skilled Helper: A Systematic Approach to Effective Helping* (Pacific Grove, CA: Brooks/Cole, 1990) 61-74; H. Hackney & S. Cormier, *Counseling Strategies and Interventions*, 4th ed. (Needham Heights, MA: Allyn & Bacon, 1994) 8.

[4] Hackney & Cormier, *Counseling Strategies and Interventions*, 8.

[5] Ibid.

Understanding Crisis Intervention

Although Gerald had been a minister for a number of years, he had rarely felt more challenged by the needs of his congregation. One tragic event followed another tragic event. Even Gerald began to wonder when the challenges would end. He knew that many members of his congregation were dealing with heartbreaking situations. The newspaper was filled with the stories.

February 18: ***Mother, Two Daughters Die in Auto Accident***

Maria Salinas, and her two daughters, Crystal, age 7, and Chandra, age 5, were pronounced dead at University Hospital yesterday at 2:00 p.m. Juan Salinas, Maria's husband, and their 9-year-old son, Marcus, both survived the accident and are in stable condition at University Hospital. Police are investigating the accident. Witnesses report that Salinas's Toyota was forced off the road by a Ford Explorer in what apparently was an incident of road rage.

March 3: ***Drainage Ditch Collapses, Kills Two***

The drainage ditch at the intersection of I-40 and Broadway collapsed while construction workers were trying to repair it. Four workers were inside the drainage ditch and were required to work in a protective box. Apparently, the workers were outside the protective box when the collapse began. The four men tried to run back to the box. Two reached it while two did not. Rescue crews worked 15 hours to dig out the bodies of the two deceased workers.

May 21: ***Good Samaritan Injured in Hit and Run***

A speeding pickup hit Greg Johnson, a 45-year-old man who stopped to assist survivors of an automobile accident on a farm road. The driver of the pickup sped past the accident and left Johnson critically injured. The driver in the hit-and-run incident has not been apprehended.

June 28: *Toddler Drowns during Family Gathering*
A two-year-old boy drowned yesterday afternoon in a private pool. The boy apparently wandered away from a family gathering, entered a neighbor's backyard, and fell into an in-ground pool. When the boy was found, family members performed CPR. The boy was declared dead at University Hospital.

While each of these heartbreaking situations left individuals devastated, they also had opened doors for Gerald to minister to individuals and families. Maria Salinas's brother and his family attended Gerald's church and called and ask Gerald to meet with Juan and Marcus Salinas. Abdul Jackson, one of the two survivors of the drainage ditch collapse, was a member of Gerald's congregation. Greg Johnson and his family were active members of Gerald's church. Gerald had not anticipated being involved with the family of the toddler who drowned, but the family did not attend church anywhere and the funeral director had asked him to speak at the funeral.

While each of these devastating situations was different in some ways, Gerald was struck by how similar some aspects of the family reactions were. They endured flashbacks and nightmares, were emotionally restricted, and seemed unable to move on after the traumas they endured. Although Gerald recognized the similarities, he didn't know that he was witnessing typical responses to crisis situations.

Defining Crisis

Crisis situations are uniquely demanding for counselors. Crises are usually time-limited, persisting for a maximum of six to eight weeks. After six to eight weeks, the client's discomfort diminishes, and he or she is able to return to daily functioning. What occurs during the immediate aftermath of the crisis event determines whether or not the client will be able to return to healthy daily functioning or will continue to exhibit long-term and chronic emotional difficulties. Although clients may resolve the original crisis situation, it is not uncommon for stressful situations to bring the client to a crisis state again.

A crisis can be defined in several ways. When individuals do not know how to respond to a situation, a crisis occurs.[1] When people cannot use their customary methods of problem-solving to overcome a situation or obstacle, a period of disorganization begins.[2] Because individuals do not know how to respond, the crisis situation immobilizes people and prevents them from making conscious choices to control their lives.[3]

What is most interesting about crisis situations is that no particular situation creates a crisis for everyone. Indeed, some individuals may cope with seeming ease with situations that leave others immobilized and unable to make even minor decisions. The core of effective crisis intervention is recognizing that the situation itself does not necessarily create a crisis, rather the way people react to a situation may cause a crisis.[4] The disruption in coping mechanisms and the feelings of shock and distress are about how people react to a particular situation rather than about the situation itself. A crisis is the perception that a situation is an intolerable difficulty that exceeds a person's ability to cope.[5]

Applying What You Know

Remember not everyone responds to the same situations in the same way. It is a person's reaction to a situation that creates a crisis, not the situation itself. Place a check by the following situations that are crises.

_____ 1. Following a traffic accident, a paramedic finds a young boy whose hand has been severed. The paramedic immediately mobilizes to care for the victim. After the boy is safely transported to the emergency room, the paramedic takes another call and continues to work his shift. He does not experience nightmares or flashbacks. Medical emergencies are a daily part of his life.

_____ 2. A man divorces his wife after 22 years of marriage. She is devastated. She refuses to leave her house and does not answer her phone. She lies on the couch all day in the dark. She hasn't eaten in three days.

_____ 3. A tornado rips through a farmer's land destroying his crop and his home. The farmer and his family escape unharmed. However, the farmer sits on his wrecked tractor looking out on his land and has not spoken with the insurance adjuster.

_____ 4. A teenage driver is broadsided by a van. The van completely totals the car the teenager is driving. The teen is angry about the damage to the car but isn't afraid to drive again.

_____ 5. A man pulls a gun in a bank and demands that the teller fill a bag with money. The teller complies with the request. Another teller recognizes what is happening and notifies the police. The police apprehend the bank robber just outside the bank. During the weeks following the bank robbery, the teller is unable to return to work at the bank.

Answers

Situations **one** and **four** are **not** crisis situations because the individuals did not perceive the situations to be crises, even though we might perceive them to be. When individuals have the coping skills to deal with a trauma, it does not necessarily become a crisis situation.

Characteristics of Crisis Situations

Understanding what situations create a crisis is the first step in providing effective counseling. The second step is recognizing the characteristics of crisis situations. Although we tend to view crisis situations as having negative outcomes, they also provide a chance for individuals to grow and emerge from the experience changed in positive ways. The characteristics of crisis situations include the following:[6]

★ *Presence of danger and opportunity:* We tend to immediately recognize the danger in crisis situations. Crisis situations overwhelm people's abilities to cope and may lead them to making decisions that create emotional, physical, or spiritual harm. However, in every crisis situation, there is an opportunity for growth. When someone learns the new coping skills and problem-solving strategies to deal with a situation that they did not have the skills to deal with before, they have used an opportunity for growth.

★ *Complicated symptoms:* Because crisis situations are complicated, the symptoms of crises are complicated as well.[7] In responding to crisis, there are no simple cause-and-effect scenarios. Crisis situations resemble tangled webs with complex lines crisscrossing all different environments and people.[8] In some crisis environments such as natural disasters or wars, everyone in a community or region may be impacted by the event in different ways.

★ *Seeds of growth and change:* The anxiety that is created in crisis situations may provide an impetus for change. When we are comfortable in our environment, we tend to be complacent and content with ourselves and our lives. Crisis can force us to change and grow.

★ *No quick fixes:* Although crises may develop quickly, the distress and discomfort created by crises are rarely fixed quickly. While some of the problematic reactions to a crisis may be addressed in a relatively short period of time, other symptoms may take longer to address. While crises can produce growth and change, they also produce the need to grieve the loss of what existed prior to the crisis.

★ *The necessity of choice:* Crisis situations do not allow the luxury of not making a choice. During a crisis, not choosing is making a choice. Generally, not choosing during a crisis situation leads to negative results. Choosing to do something during a crisis sets the stage for growth and change in a positive direction.[9]

★ *Universality and idiosyncrasy:* While everyone will ultimately experience crisis situations at some time in their lives, no two persons will respond to a crisis in exactly the same way.

Therefore, crisis is universal in creating disorganization for everyone, and it is idiosyncratic in the way everyone responds uniquely to a crisis.

Types of Crises

Certainly, there are common characteristics of all crisis situations, but there are unique characteristics of crises related to the type of situation that occurs. Some crisis situations develop abruptly without any ability to anticipate the onset, while there may be crises where there are forewarnings of impending challenges. Table 4.1 outlines four general types of crises.[10]

Type	Description	Examples
Developmental	An event in the normal flow of human life that causes a dramatic change that produces abnormal responses. These crises are considered normal.	Birth of a child Graduating from college Career changes Retirement
Situational	The occurrence of an uncommon or extraordinary event that an individual cannot control or forecast. These events are random, sudden, shocking, and intense.	Terrorist attacks Automobile accidents Kidnappings Rapes Sudden illness or death
Existential	Crisis occurring as the result of inner conflicts and anxieties related to issues of purpose, responsibility, independence, freedom, and commitment.	Realization that one will never make a significant impact Remorse that one never married A void that can never be filled in a meaningful way
Environmental	Crisis occurring when some natural or human-caused disaster strikes a person or group of people. This type of crisis may affect virtually every member of the environment.	Hurricanes Floods or tidal waves Volcanic eruptions Tornadoes Famine Forest Fires

Table 4.1 Crisis Types

Applying What You Know

Using the information provided in the previous chart, identify what type of crisis situation each of the following narratives describes.

A=Developmental

B=Situational

C=Existential

D=Environmental

_____ 1. A construction worker is on-site when a drainage ditch collapses. He ran to a protective box and survived the collapse. He heard the screams of two coworkers who died in the collapse. He stayed on-site while rescue workers dug for 15 hours to recover the bodies of the deceased workers. As a result of the experience, he is having nightmares and flashbacks.

_____ 2. A man divorces his wife after 22 years of marriage. She is devastated. She refuses to leave her house and does not answer her phone. She lies on the couch all day in the dark. She hasn't eaten in three days.

_____ 3. A tornado rips through a farmer's land destroying his crop and his home. The farmer and his family escape unharmed. However, the farmer sits on his wrecked tractor looking out on his land and has not spoken with the insurance adjuster.

_____ 4. A wife and mother begins corresponding on the Internet with a man living in another state. After several months of Internet correspondence, she packs her bags one day and leaves her family to go live with this man. When her husband tries to persuade her to come home, she tells him that she doesn't feel fulfilled as a wife and mother and she doesn't want to return.

_____ 5. A man pulls a gun in the bank and demands that the teller fill a bag with money. The teller complies with the

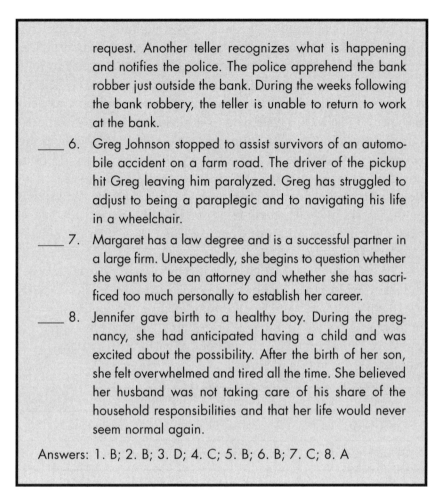

request. Another teller recognizes what is happening and notifies the police. The police apprehend the bank robber just outside the bank. During the weeks following the bank robbery, the teller is unable to return to work at the bank.

_____ 6. Greg Johnson stopped to assist survivors of an automobile accident on a farm road. The driver of the pickup hit Greg leaving him paralyzed. Greg has struggled to adjust to being a paraplegic and to navigating his life in a wheelchair.

_____ 7. Margaret has a law degree and is a successful partner in a large firm. Unexpectedly, she begins to question whether she wants to be an attorney and whether she has sacrificed too much personally to establish her career.

_____ 8. Jennifer gave birth to a healthy boy. During the pregnancy, she had anticipated having a child and was excited about the possibility. After the birth of her son, she felt overwhelmed and tired all the time. She believed her husband was not taking care of his share of the household responsibilities and that her life would never seem normal again.

Answers: 1. B; 2. B; 3. D; 4. C; 5. B; 6. B; 7. C; 8. A

Characteristics Unique to Crisis Situations

Although there are some universal helping skills that must be mastered to be effective in all counseling situations, there are some unique skills that are necessary to be effective in crisis situations. First, you must be able to deal with a problem that has a sudden and dramatic onset. In crisis situations, you frequently have no indications that a crisis is developing or impending. Therefore, you must have the flexibility to respond to a very sudden and frequently devastating situation without it alarming you as the counselor.

The sheer devastation of some crisis situations can be difficult for a counselor to handle, but in addition to the crisis situation itself, you must assist individuals in the chaos of a crisis. Emotions are frequently volatile in crisis situations, and you need to be able to assess what is causing the emotional response and how to help the client find a way to cope with overwhelming emotion. You cannot feed the emotional reaction; you have to be calm and help the client begin to calm down and cope with the situation. In addition, you cannot let the intensity of the emotions in a crisis situation startle you or intimidate you. If you are overwhelmed by the intense emotions of the client, it will reinforce his or her sense of helplessness. Even if you don't know what to do in a crisis situation, remain calm and reassuring.

During a crisis people can be completely out of control because they have no coping skills for the situation. A crisis disrupts the client's mobility and equilibrium creating disequilibrium and immobility (defined in Table 4.2[11]). Quite literally, a crisis situation can leave an individual frozen and out of balance with no idea how to regain movement and balance.

Term	Definition
Equilibrium	A state of mental or emotional stability and balance.
Disequilibrium	Lack of mental or emotional stability and balance
Mobility	Being flexible or adaptable to the physical and social world
Immobility	Unable to adapt to the immediate physical and social world.

Table 4.2

In the immediate aftermath of a crisis, it is not likely that the client will develop new coping skills, so you will need to be directive and tell them what they need to do to handle the immediate aftermath of the crisis. Directive interventions need to be limited to the first few days following a crisis situation. The quickest way to get the client to become mobile is to facilitate positive actions that the client can take at once. People who successfully cope with crisis experiences report that the most helpful intervention during a crisis is to engage in some concrete and immediate activity. It may be very difficult for immobilized people to take independent and autonomous action even though that is what they need to do most. The fundamental problem in immobility is loss of control. When the client becomes involved in doing something concrete which is a step in a positive direction, an element of control is restored, a degree of mobility is provided, and the climate for forward movement is established. A sign of progress for clients is when they are able to regain their ability to cope with the stressors associated with daily functioning and integrating the trauma into their lives.

Time is critical in crisis intervention. You don't have the luxury of having several sessions to gather background information before setting goals. You are forced to make decisions on available information. You have to quickly assess the situation and determine how to intervene. Furthermore, crisis situations are constantly emerging and changing, thus requiring constant time-urgent decisions.

Ultimately, in all crisis situations, you must believe the client can be pulled through the crisis. Your resolve that the client can pull through the situation may be the constant reassurance the client needs to be able to move forward and make decisions when they seem to have no hope. If you have trouble believing that a client will pull through a situation, remember that we are all created in God's image, and with God's help we can accomplish immeasurably more than we recognize.

Wrapping It Up

Hopefully the information provided in this chapter will help you begin to conceptualize the effects of crisis situations. Keep in mind that crisis situations can create immediate chaos and immobilization, but many of the effects of a crisis get better in six to eight weeks. While the impact of a crisis may diminish in a short period of time, it is important to provide effective interventions to help prevent the development of long-term emotional issues related to the trauma.

Chapter Four References

[1] R.R. Carkhuff & B.G. Berensen, *Beyond Counseling and Therapy* (New York: Holt, Rinehart, & Winston, 1977) 165.

[2] G. Caplan, *An Approach to Community Mental Health* (New York: Grune & Stratton, 1961) 18.

[3] G. Belkin, *Introduction to Counseling,* 2nd ed. (Dubuque, IA: W.C. Brown, 1984) 424.

[4] L.M. Brammer, *The Helping Relationship: Process and Skills* (Englewood Cliffs, NJ: Prentice-Hall, 1985) 94.

[5] James & Gilliland, *Crisis Intervention Strategies,* 3.

[6] Ibid.

[7] Brammer, *The Helping Relationship,* 91; G. Kliman, *Crisis Psychological First Aid for Recovery and Growth* (New York: Holt Rinehart, & Winston, 1978) xxi.

[8] James & Gilliland, *Crisis Intervention Strategies,* 4.

[9] Ibid., 5

[10] Ibid.

[11] Ibid., 22

Understanding Life Transitions

Roy and Roxanne planned for their retirement for years. Roy had worked as a mechanical engineer in the oil field, and Roxanne had been a teacher's assistant at school. They had spent the last thirty years living in a small town pinching pennies and investing conservatively. Despite the ups and downs of oil field employment, Roy had maintained steady work throughout his career. Sometimes it didn't pay as well as it did at other times, but it had always paid the bills. Because of their conservative approach to spending and their commitment to saving for retirement, both Roy and Roxanne retired when they were 52.

They both had anticipated traveling and pursuing recreational and leisure activities when they retired. For the first eighteen months after they retired, they traveled to the places they had dreamed of seeing. As much as they enjoyed the traveling, they grew tired of living out of their suitcases. By the time they were 54, they were spending the majority of their time back home. They began to argue with one another and were unhappy living together. By the time Roy came to talk to Gerald, Roxanne was threatening to divorce him. Gerald couldn't understand why Roy and Roxanne were having marital difficulties. Since they had retired, they were getting to relax and spend time together. Admittedly, they hadn't been as involved in church activities since their retirement, but he thought that was because of their traveling and other pursuits.

Gerald called a colleague and began describing the situation. The colleague asked several questions about Roy and Roxanne's retirement plans and what had changed between them since they had both retired. Gerald began to recognize that several things had changed that might have placed more stress on their marriage including:

★ They were spending significantly more time together.
★ Neither of them were pursuing outside recreational activities.
★ Neither of them had established a support network since they had retired.
★ Most of their friends had been involved in their work settings, and they missed the social aspects of working.
★ They had no sense of meaning or purpose in their lives— they missed contributing to the world.

Fortunately, Gerald was able to meet with Roy and Roxanne together and persuade Roxanne to work on salvaging their marriage. Both Roy and Roxanne reported being satisfied with their marriage prior to retirement, but indicated that their expectations for their marriage had changed once they had retired. Through counseling, Roy and Roxanne were able to develop more realistic expectations for their marriage as they developed some understanding of the transitions that had been created with retirement. They both began to volunteer with separate organizations and spent more time developing closer friendships at church. When they were together, they had more to share about their lives because they were both actively involved in outside volunteer and leisure activity. If Gerald had not recognized the transitional issues in Roy and Roxanne's life, he might have focused his counseling strategies on relational issues without addressing the ultimate life stressor.

Roy and Roxanne experienced some drastic changes in their lives. If we are honest with ourselves, we will recognize that change is constant in our lives as well. We experience changes in our jobs, our families, our health, and our relationships. Changes make it difficult for us to make short-term or long-term plans. We even experience changes in our relationship with God if we are growing and studying His word. While God is a constant in our lives, our spiritual growth should create changes in how we relate to God. The one constant we can depend on is change. While we all experience changes, we often may have difficulty with transitions created by change.

Differences between Changes and Transitions

What's the difference between changes and transitions? A *change* is a shift in external conditions such as a new boss, a promotion, a new home, etc. A *transition* is what goes on inside of you in response to the change.

★ A transition involves disengaging from the old way of doing things and the old identity you had.

★ A transition includes going through a confusing in-between time.

★ A successful transition requires becoming comfortable with the new way of doing things and the new identity that you are developing.

Transitions actually "start with an ending and finish with a beginning."[1] With change you focus on the outcome the change produces. With transition you focus on the ending you'll have to make to leave an old situation behind. Transition starts with an ending. Even in good changes, there are transitions where you begin by letting go of something. Regardless of who we are, we experience transitions in life. Because few of us are prepared for transitions or recognize how transitions impact us, frequently clients are dealing with issues related to transitions. Understanding the basic types of transitions is the foundation of helping clients deal with transitions. There are three general categories of transitions: environmental transitions, life development transitions, and relationship transitions. The characteristics of each of these types of transitions will be discussed in this chapter.

Recognizing Environmental Transitions

When we think of transitions, we probably initially think of environmental transitions. Environmental transitions are transitions that are initiated by changes in our external environments. Environmental transitions may be planned and expected or sudden and unexpected. Even with anticipated transitions, there are adjustment issues and losses to be addressed. For example, you may be very excited about moving to a new house, but the move itself is stressful because it messes up your daily routine. In addition, if you have lived in a house for a period of years, you may discover that you feel saddened about leaving the house although you want to move to the new house. Moving from the old house provokes memories of the shared experiences you had in the house, and you grieve leaving the house and what it represents.

Environmental transitions vary in the degree of stress they produce. Examples of environmental transitions include:

★ Divorce
★ Moving to a new city
★ Death of a loved one
★ Loss of a job
★ Changing jobs or bosses
★ Experiencing legal difficulties
★ Financial problems
★ Retirement
★ Marriage

Applying What You Know

1. What environmental transitions have you experienced in the last three years? _____

_____

_____

_____

2. How well did you cope with these environmental stressors?

_____

_____

_____

_____

3. What strategies did you use to cope with these environmental transitions? _____

_____

_____

_____

4. What environmental stressors would be most difficult for
   you to handle? _____

_____

_____

_____

_____

Recognizing Developmental Transitions

Until recently we thought of children and adolescents experiencing developmental changes and transitions. The assumption was that adults changed little and faced few transitions until they became old. Little thought was given to changes that occurred between adolescence and old age. Since there were no obvious signs of growth or decline during most of the adulthood years, any changes or transitions were primarily related to external events like death of a spouse or loss of a job. People were expected to become mature, responsible citizens living productive lives. When problems and difficulties occurred, they were not seen as being related to lifespan development. In recent years, we have learned that there are several life transitions in adulthood that may not be related to external circumstances, but are related to lifespan development. Table 5.1 outlines some common life transitions. The dark gray portions of the table represent transitions, while the light gray represent stages.

Age	Stage	Tasks
16 to 22	Leaving the Family	Terminate pre-adulthood and take preliminary steps into the adult world. Explore possibilities and make tentative commitments.
22 to 28	Entering the Adult World	Create a first major life structure, which may include marriage and a separate home, a mentoring relationship, and the dream. Attempt to pursue the dream.
28 to 33	Age Thirty Transition	Become aware of the flaws of first life structure and reassess it. Reconsider earlier choices and make new ones as needed.
33 to 40	Settling Down	Create a second adult life structure; invest oneself in work, family, friendships, community. Establish a place in society and strive to "make it," to achieve the dream.
40 to 45	Mid-Life Transition	A bridge from early to middle adulthood. Deciding what one has done with his/her life and what he/she wants to do. May or may not involve crisis.
45 to 50	Entering Middle Adulthood	Create a new life structure, often with a new job, new marriage, or change in work life.
50 to 55	Age 50 Transition	A minor adjustment to the middle adult life structure. However, if no crisis occurred at the mid-life transition, it is more likely to occur now.
55 to 60	Culmination of Middle Adulthood	Build a second midlife structure, analogous to settling down in middle adulthood. May be a particularly satisfying time if the adult has successfully adapted the life structures to changes in roles and self.
60 to 65	Late Adult Transition	Termination of middle adulthood and bridge to late adulthood. Conclude the efforts of middle adulthood, prepare for retirement and the physical declines of old age. A major turning point in the life cycle.
65 +	Late Adulthood	Create a new life structure that will suit the new patterns in retirement and increasing physical declines. Cope with illness. Deal with the issue of loss of youth.

Table 5:1 Life Stages[2]

In addition to experiencing life stage transitions, there are periods of time in life, like retirement, when people generally move through a series of stages and transitions as they adjust to changes in their lives. Table 5.2 outlines the phases of retirement.

Stage	Characteristics
Preretirement Phase	Individual becomes aware that retirement is approaching and saves money, dreams of things to do, and prepares for the transition.
Honeymoon Phase	Immediately after retirement, the retiree enjoys the free time and starts doing things he or she has waited years to do.
Disenchantment Phase	The retiree begins to feel depressed about life and the lack of things to do. The individual completes things he or she has wanted to do for years and gets tired and bored.
Reorientation Phase	The individual reevaluates decisions about activities in retirement and develops a more realistic attitude toward effective use of time.
Stability Phase	The retirement routine is established and enjoyed. The routine keeps the retiree happy and feeling that his or her life has meaning.
Terminal Phase	Illness or disability prevents the retiree from actively taking care of himself or the retiree reenters the work force

Table 5.2 Phases of Retirement[3]

Applying What You Know

1. Do you think that these life stages are accurate? Have you seen them in your life or in the lives of people close to you?

   _____

   _____

   _____

   _____

   _____

2. When you look at these life stages, which transitions would you anticipate being the most difficult for you? Why?

_____

_____

_____

_____

3. In examining the phases of retirement, why do you think retirement is more difficult for some individuals than for others? _____

_____

_____

_____

4. What do you expect to do when you retire? Relax? Start a second career? Travel? How do these expectations impact the transition to retirement? _____

_____

_____

_____

Recognizing Relationship Transitions

Relationship transitions provide challenges for all the individuals in the relationship. When two people get married, it affects both of them and their extended families as well. When a couple has children, it impacts both of them, the child, and often extended families, colleagues, and friends. Relationship transitions happen in marriages, families, and parenting. In addition, relationship transitions occur as an individual makes career advancements or changes at work and when individuals divorce or when grandparents take on the role of parenting their grandchildren. Table 5.3 outlines the stages of the family life cycle and Table 5.4 outlines the phases of parenting.

Family Stage	Key Principles	Changes in Family Status
Leaving Home	Accepting emotional and financial responsibility for self	Establish self independent from family Develop intimate peer relationships Establish work and financial independence
The New Couple	Commitment to new family system	Establish marital relationship Realign relationships with extended family and friends to include spouse
Family of Young Children	Accept new members into the family	Adjust marriage to make space for children Cooperation in parenting, finances, and household tasks Realign relationships with extended family to include parent and grandparent roles
Family of Adolescents	Increase flexibility of family roles to accommodate growing independence of adolescents	Shift parenting relationship to allow the adolescent to establish identity Refocus on marital or career issues Begin shift toward caring for older generation in family
Launching Children	Accepting exits and entrances into the family as children establish independence and begin their own families	Reestablishing emphasis on marital relationship without parenting role Develop adult-to-adult relationships with children Realign family roles to include in-laws and grandchildren Deal with disabilities and death of parents and/or grandparents
Later Life Family	Accepting the shifting of generational roles	Maintain personal and marital independence with physical decline Support for a more central role for the middle generation Make room in the system for the wisdom and experience of the elderly Support elderly family members without taking over tasks and roles they can still manage Deal with the loss of spouse, siblings, and other peers Prepare for own death through reviewing one's life

Table 5.3 Stages of the Family Life Cycle[4]

Stage	Age of Children	Characteristics
Parental Image Stage	Birth of first child	Mothers and fathers form images of themselves as parents, desire perfection, yet often experience unexpected heavy demands.
Nurturing Stage	Infancy	Attachment to child occurs, relationships with other people are challenged by changes to accommodate child, and heavy demands on parents.
Authority Stage	2 to 4 years old	Parents question their effectiveness as children begin to develop independence and make more demands on parents' time; often additional children are added to the family.
Integrative Stage	Preschool to Middle Childhood	Children develop more autonomy and social skills, so parents are required to set realistic goals, motivate the children, develop effective communication skills, and establish authority.
Independent Teenage Stage	Adolescents	Adolescents wrestle with identification, responsibility, and maturity. Parents provide support for their adolescents while maintaining authority and responsibility.
Departure Stage	Young Adulthood	Parents evaluate their past performance and prepare for future relationships.

Table 5.4 Stages of Parenting[5]

Dealing with Transitions

A transition ultimately involves dealing with the limbo between an old sense of identity and a new sense of identity. It is the time when the old way of doing things is gone but the new way of doing things doesn't feel comfortable yet. The gap between the old and the new is the time when innovation is most possible. Old and maladaptive patterns are replaced with new ones that are better adapted to the world in which we find ourselves. Remember, there are the following three steps to a transition:

★ A transition involves disengaging from the old way of doing things and the old identity you had.

★ A transition includes going through a confusing in-between time.

★ A successful transition requires becoming comfortable with the new way doing things and the new identity that you are developing.[6]

Coping with transitions requires that both you and your clients recognize that you have to deal with an ending before you can move on to a beginning. During a transition, people need the freedom to grieve what they are losing. They may need to verbally express their feelings about the loss, their fears, and even their resentments about the loss. Part of grieving is acknowledging the positive aspects of what you are ending in your life and openly honoring what you appreciate about that experience in your life. Then you can begin to acknowledge that there are open spaces in your life now that can be filled with new possibilities. Once you are able to recognize the opportunities for new possibilities, you can begin to examine what new actions you can take. You can go forward with your life. As a counselor, your role is to help clients recognize these aspects of moving through a transition.[7]

Wrapping It Up

Understanding how transitions impact clients and members of your congregation will help you begin to conceptualize the issues of life transitions and congregational transitions differently. If you understand the impact of transitions, you will be able to more effectively help clients become better at helping themselves and at recognizing opportunities and ways to more effectively utilize their God-given talents and abilities in the service of God's kingdom even during times of transition.[8]

_____

Chapter Five References

[1] W. Bridges, *Managing Transitions: Making the Most of Change* (Reading, MA: Addison-Wesley, 1991) 5.

[2] Daniel Levinson, *The Seasons of a Man's Life* (New York: Knopf, 1978).

[3] R. Atchley, *Social Forces and Aging: An Introduction to Social Gerontology* (Belmont, CA: Wadsworth, 1985).

[4] E.A. Carter & M. McGoldrick, *The Changing Family Life Cycle: A Framework for Family Therapy* (Boston: Allyn and Bacon, 1989).

[5] E. Galinsky, *Between Generations: The Six Stages of Parenthood* (New York: Time Books, 1981).

[6] Bridges, *Managing Transitions*, 5.

[7] V. Satir, *The New Peoplemaking* (Mountain View, CA: Science and Behavior Books, 1988) 342-343.

[8] Ibid.

Understanding Relationship Problems

Gerald was teaching a series of classes on using spiritual principles to guide family financial planning. Three weeks into the series, Maria came by Gerald's office to talk with him about her financial concerns. Maria began to describe her family's financial status.

"Louis and I have gotten into a lot of credit card debt. We've gotten to the point we can't make the payments. Louis has a good job, but it's not enough. Since we are so far in debt, Louis has made me go back to work and take two jobs to pay off the debt. I know that what we are doing will get us out of debt, but I resent having to work two jobs while Louis works one job and has the weekends off to hang out with his friends while I am working."

Gerald wasn't surprised that Maria and Louis were in debt, but he was astonished that Louis was expecting his wife to work two jobs and shoulder more of the responsibility for getting them out of credit card debt. As Gerald listened to Maria describe her schedule and stressors, he became more sympathetic toward her and more annoyed by Louis's lack of motivation in helping Maria address their financial issues.

Maria shared with Gerald that she and Louis sought out the help of a nonprofit credit counseling agency to help them figure out a way to get out of debt. Based on the current plan, it will take Maria and Louis nearly three more years to get out of debt if Maria continued to work two jobs while Louis worked one job. Louis was making considerably more money than Maria and could make more than Maria was making if he took a second job. Maria reported that Louis was unwilling to take a second job.

Gerald encouraged Maria and suggested that he meet with Louis to discuss the situation and then the three of them would get together to work out the differences in their approach to paying off debt. Gerald called Louis and set up a meeting for the next week. During the week, Gerald found himself reflecting on Louis and Maria's situation. Every time he thought of them, he felt sympathy for Maria and more and more anger toward Louis.

When Louis came to Gerald's office to meet with him, Gerald was prepared to confront Louis about placing unfair responsibilities on Maria. As the conversation progressed, Gerald began to recognize that he did not have all the information he needed about the situation. Louis described how he and Maria got into so much credit card debt.

"When Maria and I married, she had never lived away from her parents and had never had to manage money. During the first year, she spent money without realizing we didn't have the money to spend. She would overdraft our bank account and run up huge credit card bills. We nearly had to declare bankruptcy. I worked two and three jobs for four years to pay off all of the debt. Eventually, I thought I had managed to get us debt free."

Gerald realized now that Maria had only presented one side of the situation. He encouraged Louis to continue.

"While I was working these jobs to get us of debt, Maria no longer had access to our joint banking account or our credit cards. Her spending seemed to slow down. I thought things were going really well. What I didn't know was that Maria had taken out new credit cards in her name and was continuing to run up charges on those new credit cards."

"So Maria was charging items on credit cards you didn't even know she had?" asked Gerald.

"Yes. When I found out that she had been running up new credit card bills while I was working two and three jobs to pay off the previous credit card bills, I was ready to divorce Maria. When I calmed down, I agreed to go to a credit counseling agency with

Maria. The credit counseling agency worked out a plan to repay the debt. I told Maria that I would continue to pay for our household expenses, but that she would have to go to work to pay back the credit card debts she created."

At this point, Gerald recognized that the situation was more complicated than he had realized and that Maria had only presented one side of the story. He felt exasperated because he did not recognize earlier that every relationship issue has two sides to it. He realized that he had been quick to take sides in the situation rather than waiting to hear both sides of the story.

As a minister, the issues you will encounter most frequently in your counseling role will be relationship issues. Interestingly, relationship issues can seem to be the most straightforward counseling issues when they are actually the most complex issues you will address. In relationship issues, you must recognize that whoever is coming to see you in counseling is only presenting his or her side of the story. One side of the story is almost always biased and limited by a single viewpoint.

Obviously, family relationships make up the bulk of our relationship issues, but we also maintain a number of relationships at church and work as well. Interestingly, our fundamental relationship skills and styles that we use in our families carry over into relationships in other areas. We don't generally interact in relationships one way at home and a different way at work. If we have poor relationship skills, we will probably have problems with relationships in all aspects of our lives although these problems may manifest themselves in different ways. As problems manifest themselves, we need to have an awareness that emotional issues from past relationships impact the current relationship issue.

Components of Relationships

In healthy relationships, individuals are committed to helping provide what is in the best interest of the other person in the relationship. As a result, individuals in healthy relationships cooperate rather than compete, empower rather than overpower, and view problems as opportunities for change and growth. When people value and respect themselves, relationships can develop that provide the healthy support of loving, valuing, and respecting the other person. Ultimately, healthy relationships can help us understand our uniqueness and allow us to reflect God's purpose in our lives.[1]

At the core of all relationships are four basic components. These components exist in all relationships. The four concepts are:[2]

★ *Self-worth:* The feelings and ideas one has about oneself.
★ *Communication:* The ways people use to work out meaning with one another.
★ *Family system:* The rules people use for how they should feel and act.
★ *Link to Society:* The way people relate to other people and institutions outside the family.

When relationships are healthy, all four of these components in the relationship are healthy as well. In unhealthy relationships, at least one of these components is unhealthy. Table 6.1 describes these four fundamental components:

Component	Healthy	Unhealthy
Self-worth	High	Low
Communication	Direct, clear, specific, and honest	Indirect, vague, and not really honest
Family Systems	Flexible, human, appropriate, and subject to change	Rules are rigid, inhuman, non-negotiable, and everlasting
Link to Society	Open, hopeful, and based on choice	Fearful, placating, and blaming

Table 6.1 Components of Relationships[3]

Family of Origin

Our family of origin impacts the way we interact in relationships throughout our lifespan. Our family of origin includes our parents, our siblings, and our grandparents, aunts, uncles, cousins, etc. Keep in mind that parents themselves are someone's children, even when they are adults, and that they are still part of their own sibling systems even after marriage. Gaining a better understanding of the interactions in our family of origin can significantly impact the resolution of problems in our current relationships. The positions we occupy in our families of origin are the only thing we can never alter in our lifetime. Our position in our family of origin is the source of our uniqueness and an integral part of our emotional strengths and challenges. The more we understand our position in our family of origin, the more effectively we can interact with people in all aspects of our lives.

The worksheet below provides you with an opportunity to explore some family of origin issues for yourself. In addition, this worksheet can be used to help clients explore their families of origin.

Applying What You Know

1. In the family you grew up in, what feelings and ideas did you have about yourself? _____

   _____

   _____

   _____

   _____

   _____

2. In the family you grew up in, how did family members communicate with one another? _____

   _____

   _____

   _____

   _____

   _____

   _____

   _____

---

3. What rules were there in the family you grew up in?

_____

_____

_____

_____

_____

_____

4. How did your family interact with other individuals at school, church, or in the community? _____

_____

_____

_____

_____

_____

The Six Qualities of Strong Families

Since we learn much of how we interact with others through our interactions with our family members, it is important to understand the characteristics of healthy families and healthy family relationships. Although every family is unique, there are some common elements of all healthy families. Not every family will demonstrate all six qualities, nor is the emphasis on the qualities the same across all families. However, the following six qualities consistently appear in healthy families:[4]

1. **Appreciation:** Individuals express appreciation for each other and try to encourage one another. As a result, they build each other up spiritually and emotionally.

2. **Spending Time Together:** Strong families genuinely enjoy being together in many areas of life. They enjoy recreational time together and routine time together.

3. **Commitment:** Strong families are committed to promoting what is best for others in the family. They value the family group and want other family members to be happy. Family members are the priority for time and energy investments.

4. **Good Communication Patterns:** Healthy families spend a great deal of time talking with each other about important things, routine things, and trivial things. They use good communication to deal with life challenges and to reflect how much they enjoy spending time with each other. Family members know how to listen to others and to communicate respect. When family members argue with one another, they get angry but are able to discuss their problems and disagreements. They focus their attention on the problems rather than on one another's personal characteristics or shortcomings. They look for solutions that work for everyone and discuss solutions openly with one another.[5]

5. **Spiritual Wellness:** Healthy families are committed to a spiritual lifestyle. Many members of strong families attend organized religious services and recognize that there is a positive correlation between religion and marital happiness.[6] Strong families have an awareness of God that gives them a sense of purpose and provides support for their family.

6. **Ability to Deal with Crises:** Strong families deal with problems and crises constructively. Family members try to see positive possibilities in even the most difficult situations. In addition, they use good coping skills and communication skills to deal with crisis situations. They are supportive and unite in a crisis rather than splitting apart and attacking one another.[7]

The worksheet below provides you with an opportunity to explore some characteristics of your family structure. In addition, this worksheet can be used to help clients explore their family structure.

Based on your current family structure, respond to statements with the following scale:

1=Always   2=Usually   3=Sometimes   4=Rarely

_____ 1. Family members enjoy spending time together.

_____ 2. Our family has a strong commitment to spiritual values.

_____ 3. Family members listen to one another and respect each other.

_____ 4. Family members appreciate one another.

_____ 5. Family members spend a significant amount of time together.

_____ 6. Family members talk about disagreements and discuss their problems.

_____ 7. Family members are committed to promoting each other's happiness.

_____ 8. Family is a priority for spending time and energy.

_____ 9. Family members spend time talking about important things, functional things, and trivial things.

_____ 10. Family members discuss ways to find solutions to problems that are best for everyone.

Wrapping It Up

Despite the complexity and difficulty of relationships, we all continue to work at the relationships in our lives as we try to build healthy connections with others. We continue to reach out to others because of our common human needs:[8]

★ We need to love and be loved, to be noticed, recognized, and respected, to be literally and figuratively touched.

★ We need to matter and have a purpose.

★ We need to be stimulated and to learn new things.

★ We need to have satisfying and intimate relationships.

★ We need to have fun and humor.

★ We need to be economically secure.

★ We need to be mentally and physically healthy.

★ We need to belong.

★ We need to be part of a vital community of Christian friends and colleagues.

★ We need a spiritual connection to God.

As a minister, you will enhance the emotional and spiritual well-being of your congregation by helping individuals recognize the qualities and characteristics of healthy and unhealthy relationships. By helping individuals establish more healthy relationships on earth, you are helping them recognize the characteristics of an eternal relationship and unconditionally loving relationship with our heavenly Father. Our interactions with others are a reflection of God at work in our lives.

Chapter Six References

[1] Satir, *The New Peoplemaking*, 369-370.

[2] Ibid., 355.

[3] Adapted from ibid., 1-8.

[4] N. Stinnett & J. DeFrain, "The Healthy Family: Is It Possible?" in *The Second Handbook on Parent Education*, ed. by M. Fine, 2nd ed. (New York: Academic Press, 1989) 53-74.

[5] D. Mace & V. Mace, "Enriching Marriages: The Foundationstone of Family Strength," in *Family Strengths: Positive Models for Family Life*, ed. by N. Stinnett, B. Chesser, J. DeFrain, & P. Knaub (Lincoln, NE: University of Nebraska Press, 1980) 89-110.

[6] N. Stinnett & J. DeFrain, *Secrets of Strong Families* (Boston: Little, Brown, 1985).

[7] Stinnett & DeFrain, "The Healthy Family,"; N. Stinnett, B. Knorr, J. DeFrain, & G. Rowe, "How Strong Families Cope with Crisis," *Family Perspective* 15 (1981) 159-166.

[8] Satir, *The New Peoplemaking*, 355.

Understanding Mental Illness

Sandy had married Josh just two months before he was deployed to the Middle East for a year. When Josh returned from the deployment, he seemed moody and irritable. Sandy asked him repeatedly if he was okay. She tried to cook his favorite foods and get him involved with friends at church, but he seemed unresponsive.

One night Sandy was cold and got up to change the thermostat. When she crawled back into bed, Josh reached out and grabbed her throat in a crushing one-hand grip. Sandy managed to gasp out Josh's name and swing her arms at him. Suddenly, Josh sat up in bed and let go of Sandy's throat. Josh's hand dropped to his side, he lay back down, then rolled over with his back turned to Sandy.

Sandy's heart beat rapidly as she lay silently in bed. She replayed what had just happened and began to think she must have imagined it. For the rest of the night, her sleep was fitful and filled with dreams of Josh attacking her.

The next morning when she woke up, Josh was up and was reading the paper at the kitchen table. She almost convinced herself that she imagined Josh choking her, yet when she looked in the mirror, she saw a bruised hand print on her neck.

Sandy entered the kitchen to find Josh had finished reading the paper and was cooking breakfast. Sandy noticed the table was set with coffee and orange juice at her place. She thought that Josh must have been remorseful for choking her and was trying to make amends. Her first reaction was relief, but she quickly got angry and confronted Josh.

"Josh, cooking breakfast isn't going to change what happened last night!"

Josh, without turning around, said, "I don't know what you're talking about. I started breakfast because you were taking so long to get out of bed."

Sandy felt the anger rising in her and she angrily demanded, "What do you mean you don't know what I'm talking about? Don't stand there acting like you don't know what you did last night. Turn around and look at me."

Josh sighed, wiped his hands on a dish towel, and turned around. When Josh saw the bruising on Sandy's neck, his eyes widened in surprise.

"What happened to your neck?" he asked.

Sandy realized that Josh didn't know what happened. Sandy told Josh about how he had choked her after she got back in bed during the night. Josh had no memory of the incident at all.

After hearing what happened, Josh slowly moved to sit down in a chair and dropped his head into his hands. He shook his head repeatedly, then without saying a word walked into the bedroom and packed his clothes in a duffel bag. He walked back into the kitchen and told Sandy, "I'm leaving." Without making eye contact or saying another word, he walked out the door.

Josh rented a motel room and began to think he must be "crazy" since he couldn't remember choking Sandy. He knew that he had felt numb since returning from the Middle East, and the nightmares and flashbacks of what he witnessed in the Middle East were exhausting him emotionally. Now he felt as if he had lost it completely. He loved Sandy, but he didn't trust himself to be around her.

After isolating himself at the motel for several days, Josh decided he needed to talk to someone, and the only person he trusted was a youth minister from his hometown congregation. He called his parents and found out that Gerald became the pulpit minister at another congregation. Josh called Gerald and arranged a time to visit with him.

When Gerald met with Josh, he noticed immediately Josh's lack of emotional expression and his flat monotone as he described what happened to him. Gerald remembered the lively banter and fun-loving pranks Josh was known for in the youth group. The striking difference disturbed Gerald. He didn't want to believe that Josh was "crazy," but he didn't know what else to think. He listened attentively to Josh and assured him that he would find someone to help him.

After meeting with Josh, Gerald called a counselor at the local veteran's center and described what had been happening with Josh. The counselor reassured Gerald that what Josh was experiencing was not that unusual for military personnel who have witnessed traumatic events. He assured Gerald that he could help Josh and set up a time for Gerald to bring Josh to the veteran's center to meet him.

Several months later, Sandy phoned Gerald to thank him for helping Josh find a counselor. She reported that Josh was living back in their home and that he was having fewer nightmares and flashbacks.

Clearly Gerald recognized that Josh was experiencing difficulties that were more significant than an adjustment to returning to his civilian life. Josh's counselor diagnosed him with posttraumatic stress disorder which is a mental illness. However, a diagnosis of a mental illness does not necessarily mean that the condition will be permanent or completely disabling.

If you are going to provide counseling as a part of your ministry, you need to understand how mental illness impacts people and their immediate and extended families. Generally, mental illness is defined as "abnormal behavior." How would you define abnormal behavior? Read the examples below and decide which of these behaviors you would regard as abnormal. Please note that I'm asking you to define the behaviors as abnormal, not necessarily as morally or spiritually okay.

★ A coach who wears a "lucky" suit to important games

★ An elderly woman who gets drunk three or four times a month

★ A husband who gets angry at his wife and slams his fist through a window

★ A woman who refuses to use silverware in a restaurant and brings her own silverware with her

★ A college student who believes that the FBI has planted a radio transmitter in his brain to monitor his thoughts

★ A gymnast who does not eat for several days to try to keep her weight down for competition

★ A man who wants to kill himself because his girlfriend has broken off their relationship

★ A woman who breaks into a cold sweat when she has to speak in public

How did you decide what was normal and abnormal? What were your criteria for defining abnormal behavior? Did you just rely on your experiences or your immediate reaction without developing particular criteria? Defining abnormal behavior is difficult because what might be normal behavior in one situation may be very abnormal behavior in another situation. A behavior that in moderation may be viewed as normal may be viewed as abnormal if done to excess.

Think of abnormal behavior as occurring on a scale of 1 to 10, with 1 being normal and 10 being abnormal (see Figure 7.1). Most of us have a pretty clear idea of what behaviors are clearly normal and clearly abnormal, but it is the middle of the continuum that becomes difficult for us to define.

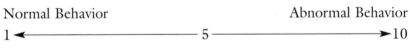

Normal Behavior   Abnormal Behavior

1 ◄───────────── 5 ──────────────► 10

Figure 7.1

Consider the example of sleep. How much sleep is normal? How much sleep is abnormal? Most of us would probably agree that between seven and nine hours of sleep is in the normal range. Not that we all get that much sleep on a regular basis, but we would not view sleeping seven to nine hours a day as abnormal. We might be able to agree that two hours of sleep a day is abnormal. But we would begin to disagree about whether only getting five to six hours of sleep is abnormal. If you need nine hours of sleep a night to function well, you might view someone who only needs five hours of sleep a day on a regular basis as abnormal. But if you only need six hours of sleep on a regular basis to function well, you might not view needing five hours of sleep a day as abnormal. Obviously, your own experiences will impact how you determine if behavior is normal or abnormal.

For counseling situations, behavior is deemed abnormal in several different ways.[1]

- *Distress* is the experience of physical or emotional pain. At times the level of pain may become so great that a person has difficulty functioning.
- *Impairment* is a reduction in a person's ability to function at an optimal or even an average level. Intense distress may lead to impairment in some instances. Interestingly enough, there may be individuals who feel they are fine and do not recognize that there is any impairment in their daily functioning.
- *Risk to self or others* refers to a danger or threat to the well-being of a person including physical or psychological welfare. Examples of risk to self or others include: suicide, abusing children, exploiting the elderly, or abusing a spouse.
- *Socially and culturally unacceptable behavior* is the final criterion for abnormal behavior. Any behavior that falls outside what is normal for our culture or society is considered to be abnormal behavior. For example, laughing throughout a funeral would generally be considered inappropriate behavior in our culture.

If we are to recognize and deal with abnormal behavior, we need to understand its causes, which usually arise out of a complex set of circumstances. Rarely is there a single cause of abnormal behavior or mental illness. There are four primary domains that contribute to mental illness: biology, psychology, spirituality, and social environment.[2] Table 7.1 outlines these four domains.

Contributor	Causes	Examples
Biology	Genetic inheritance Disturbances in physical functioning Brain damage Medication Illness	Thyroid problems Head trauma Prescribed medication Illegal drugs Exposure to toxic substances

Psychology	Distorted perceptions Faulty thinking Traumatic life experiences Learned associations	Belief that one is being persecuted Belief that one will never succeed
Spirituality	Sin leading to lack of a relationship with God	Having an affair Lying Cheating
Environment	Disturbances in intimate relationships Problems in extended relationships	Unhealthy relationships Abusive relationships Death of a child Divorce

Table 7.1 Contributors to Mental Illness[3]

With some mental illnesses it may seem that one of these areas contributes more to the development of symptoms, while with other mental illnesses it seems that other areas contribute more. For example, individuals do not develop schizophrenia unless they have inherited a genetic predisposition for it. Conversely, posttraumatic stress disorder is almost always the result of an extraordinary environmental trauma like war or rape. Some individuals can cope with the trauma without developing the disorder. Yet when the disorder does develop, it is clearly due in part to the client's environment.

A more thorough discussion of the development of mental illness is beyond the scope of this book. However, there is a general consensus that the development of mental illness is triggered by multiple factors. In most cases more than one type of contributor is involved. Mental illness may develop from environmental and spiritual situations. Or it could be genetic and psychological circumstances that lead to abnormal behavior. There is no simple cause-and-effect formula for mental illnesses.

Certainly, different types of mental illnesses will require different types of interventions.

★ If the primary cause is biological, then medical intervention is warranted. Psychiatrists are best equipped in such situations, although ministers and counselors may be needed for emotional support.

★ If the primary cause is spiritual, then a minister should take the lead.

★ If the primary cause is psychological, then a counselor or psychologist is best equipped to intervene.

Categories of Psychological Disorders

Understanding the ways a mental illness may develop is an important first step in understanding how to assist individuals with mental illnesses. However, if you are going to provide counseling for members of your congregation, you need some awareness of the scope of mental illnesses. Table 7.2 provides a brief synopsis of the categories of mental illness.

Category	Description	Examples
Mood Disorders	Disorders involving emotions	Depression Post-partum depression Bipolar Disorder Mania
Anxiety Disorders	Disorders involving intense fear, anxiety, or worry that leads to behavior to avoid or reduce the anxiety	Phobias Panic Disorder Obsessive-Compulsive Disorder Posttraumatic Stress Disorder
Eating Disorder	Disorders involving problems in eating behaviors	Anorexia Bulimia
Sleep Disorders	Disorders involving problems in sleep behaviors	Insomnia Hypersomnia Nightmare Disorder Sleepwalking Disorder
Adjustment Disorders	Disorders that begin as a maladaptive behavioral or emotional response to a significant stressor in the environment	Grief following a death Adjustment following a divorce Adjustment to career change
Substance-related Disorders	Disorders related to the use or abuse of legal or illegal substances	Cocaine addiction Alcoholism Heroin addiction Sniffing or Huffing
Impulse-Control Disorder	Disorders involving repetition of impulsive behaviors that cause harm to self or others	Kleptomania Pyromania Pathological Gambling Intermittent Explosive Disorder
Dissociative Disorders	Disorders involving an interruption in conscious awareness, memory, or identity	Amnesia Fugue Dissociative Identity Disorder

Somatoform Disorders	Disorders involving recurring complaints of physical or medical symptoms without evidence of a medical condition	Pain Disorder Hypochondriasis Pain Disorder Conversion Disorder Body Dysmorphic Disorder
Factitious Disorders	Conditions involving intentionally produced physical or psychological symptoms to play a sick role	Factitious Disorder Factitious Disorder by Proxy
Sexual & Gender Identity Disorders	Disorders involving problems in the normal expression of sexuality	Sexual dysfunction Fetishes Voyeurism Pedophilia
Childhood & Adolescent Disorders	Disorders that develop during the early years of life	Learning disorders ADHD Tic Disorders Autism
Schizophrenia & Psychotic Disorders	Disorders involving distortions in perceptions of reality	Schizophrenia Delusional Disorder Brief Psychotic Disorder
Cognitive Disorders	Disorders involving problems in thinking that are caused by substances or medical conditions	Dementia Alzheimer's Amnesia
Disorders due to medical conditions	Disorders that are caused by medical conditions	Personality change Mood disorders Sexual dysfunction

Table 7.2 Categories of Mental Illness[4]

Perhaps as you have read through this chart of mental illnesses, you are overwhelmed by the number of psychological disorders that exist. Obviously, in your role as a minister, you won't be expected to treat all these mental illnesses. However, having an awareness of the scope of these psychological issues will help you be more effective in meeting the needs of your congregation. Being able to recognize when you are working with a client who might have a mental illness will allow you to be better prepared to provide spiritual mentoring, counseling, and/or a referral to a professional with more training.

Impact on the Individual and Family

Our culture stigmatizes a person with a mental illness. A stigma is "a label that causes certain people to be regarded as different, defective, and set apart from mainstream society."[5] A large percentage of Americans are fearful of people with mental illness and do not wish to interact with them.[6] Society views individuals with mental illness as incompetent, incapable of improving, unable to live independently, crazy, out-of-control, and even violent. People with severe mental illnesses often find that other people resist living near them, socializing with them, or employing them.[7] Once people with a mental illness begin to experience being stigmatized, they often experience long-lasting emotional reactions. They may think less of themselves, be unwilling to take advantage of opportunities for growth and development, and eventually come to believe the myths of society.[8]

Often even before a person with a psychological disorder has been diagnosed, the family has been impacted. The individual with the mental illness may have already placed stress on the family system by being erratic or not properly caring for himself. The family may have withdrawn to try to mask the mental illness and its impact on the family. Because of the societal stigma directed toward mental illness, the family may be embarrassed by the individual who is struggling with a mental illness. Ironically, families often feel that the last place they can turn to for help is a church family. Frequently, families fear that the mental illness will further isolate them in a church community. Parents often blame themselves for a mental illness and may believe that if they had parented a child differently the child would not have a mental illness. Furthermore, some families believe that churches only have a place for "perfect" families, so they hide their struggles from the church.

Wrapping It Up

As a minister, you can work effectively in providing counseling and even spiritual mentoring to your church members if you do recognize when people are struggling with mental illness. Certainly a complete mastery of psychological disorders is beyond the scope of ministry.

Mental illness is strongly stigmatized in our culture and within our churches, so individuals most needing our support and assistance in dealing with mental illness may be individuals who are most marginalized from seeking our assistance. If we have the skills to recognize the symptoms of mental illness, we can reach out to individuals and families who are isolated and struggling alone.

However, having the skills to recognize mental illness and actually providing treatment for a mental illness are decidedly different skills. In fact, even professionally trained counselors may recognize certain mental illnesses and realize they do not have the skills to effectively treat individuals with those disorders. As a result, professional counselors will make referrals to other professionals who are more adequately prepared and trained to intervene with certain clients. Hopefully, you as a minister will utilize the same system. When you recognize a mental illness or maybe even suspect a mental illness, you will stop and examine your own training and skills to determine if you have the ability to assist the client. If you are like most ministers, you do not have the training to effectively intervene with clients who have a mental illness and will need to make a referral to a professional counselor.

Chapter Seven References

[1] R.P. Halgin & S.K. Whitbourne, *Abnormal Psychology: Clinical Perspectives on Psychological Disorders* (Boston: McGraw-Hill Education, 2004) 5-6.

[2] Ibid., 6-10.

[3] Ibid.

[4] Ibid., 46-47.

[5] Ibid., 28.

[6] M. Salter & P. Byrne, "The Stigma of Mental Illness: How You Can Use the Media to Reduce It," *Psychiatric Bulletin* 24 (2000) 281-283.

[7] P.W. Corrigan & D.L. Penn, "Lessons from Social Psychology on Discrediting Psychiatric Stigma," *American Psychologist* 54 (1999) 765-776; D.L. Penn & J. Martin, "The Stigma of Severe Mental Illness: Some Potential Solutions for a Recalcitrant Problem," *Psychiatric Quarterly* 69 (1998) 235-247.

[8] Wright, Gronfein, & Owens (2000) http://www.mentalhealthcommission.gov/reports/Finalreport/downloads/finalreport.pdf.

What Now?

Every September, Gerald and the leaders in his church plan a retreat to discuss issues in the church and to clarify Gerald's role and responsibilities in working with the congregation. The church leaders ask Gerald to review his roles and responsibilities in the church for the past year as part of preparing for the retreat.

Gerald began reviewing how he had spent his time during the previous year. He looked over his calendar month by month. He was surprised to find that he had been spending ten to fifteen hours a week counseling members of his congregation. He realized he was spending significantly more time counseling with individuals than he had spent in previous years.

Gerald found himself contemplating how he was spending his time in his ministry. He realized that he was spending less time preparing sermons and curriculum for Bible class. He was also interacting less with members of his congregation as a spiritual mentor because he was spending so much time counseling. He felt uncertain about whether he should continue to spend a significant amount of time counseling individuals versus spending his time on spiritual instruction and mentoring.

As he considered his investment of time in counseling, Gerald acknowledged that he was functioning in an area of ministry that he was not prepared for. He hoped and prayed that he provided insightful guidance for those who sought his counseling assistance.

However, he had no formal counseling training and had difficulty distinguishing between how he should help in relationship issues, crisis situations, and mental illness problems. He knew there were situations where he should refer people to professionals with more training, but he didn't know when and how to make those referrals.

As Gerald continued his preparation for the yearly planning retreat, he decided that he wanted input from the church leaders about his role in counseling with individuals who were members of the congregation and those who were not. Gerald wanted to pursue more training about counseling issues if he was going to continue to provide ten to fifteen hours of counseling each week. Still Gerald didn't know how counseling individuals would continue to impact the other aspects of his ministry.

Perhaps you have found yourself in the same quandary as Gerald. You have drifted into counseling as part of your ministry, and you have reached the point where you realize you have to improve your counseling skills or decide to counsel less. While it is certainly flattering for other people to turn to you for assistance and respect your words of wisdom, counseling comes at a price. Before you embrace the role of counseling as part of your ministry, consider the implications for the rest of your ministry.

1. The time you invest in counseling is time you take away from other aspects of your ministry. There are only 24 hours in any day. God holds each of us responsible for how we use our time and talent. Prayerfully consider if counseling is where God wants you and needs you to invest yourself as part of your ministry.

2. When you deal with counseling situations, you become aware of issues and situations that you might not ever deal with in other ways in your life. Counseling is the process of helping individuals sift and sort through the emotional garbage in their lives while helping them make sense of their experiences. Even individuals who train to be counselors often leave the field when they begin to deal with intense emotional situations and dysfunctional behaviors because they are overwhelmed by the negative situations they hear about in counseling.

3. Counseling with individuals in your congregation will place you in the position of having significantly more knowledge about

the dysfunctional and sinful behaviors of your congregation. This knowledge may make it difficult for you to deal with individuals in other contexts in your congregation.

4. Similarly, when you begin to hear stories of dysfunctional and sinful behavior on a daily basis, it may, and probably will, impact how you interact with others. Be cautious and guard against becoming so immersed in helping others through counseling that it impacts your family and personal relationships in a negative way.

5. Counseling requires confidentiality. What you hear about in a counseling context cannot be shared with others. Carefully consider your ability to hear about difficult and traumatic situations without being able to discuss the situations with other people.

6. If you feel called to counseling as a ministry, take time to consider leaving ministry and moving into the counseling profession full-time. If you aren't willing to make this transition, consider carefully your reasons for staying in a paid ministry role rather than a paid counseling role.

Even if you do not intend for counseling to be a significant part of your ministry, you will have members of your congregation seek you out for advice and consultation. Improving your knowledge of counseling issues and skills will improve your ability to meet the needs of your congregation. Gaining counseling skills and knowledge will help you recognize when you are dealing with issues that need to be referred to a professional counselor or when you are dealing with issues that you can address in a ministry role.

Let's return to Gerald's situation. When Gerald met with his church leaders during the retreat, he presented the information about how much time he was spending in counseling and his concerns about his ability to meet the needs of individuals who were seeking him out for counseling. After prayer and discussion, Gerald and the church leaders jointly decided for Gerald to restrict his counseling interventions to only members of the congregation and to limit his counseling time to 5 to 10 hours a week. In order for Gerald to limit his counseling time, he would have to make decisions about referring some individuals to other professionals rather than talking with them himself. The leaders of the church also encouraged Gerald to continue to seek out additional information and training about counseling to improve his ability to provide counseling services.

If like Gerald, you want to improve your ability to effectively intervene in crisis intervention, life transitions, relationship problems, and mental illness, you will benefit from seeking out additional training and continuing to study about counseling. Regrettably, more and more members of our congregations will need to have access to ministers who can provide godly guidance in dealing with emotional issues and relationship problems. You face the challenge of improving your ability to assist your congregation. I hope you will prayerfully and purposefully take action to improve your counseling skills.

Glossary of Terms

Accurate communication: The ability to understand the communication of the client through clarifying and restating what you hear and assessing whether the client has understood your communication as well.

Adjustment disorders: Disorders that begin as a maladaptive behavioral or emotional response to a significant stressor in the environment.

Adolescent disorders: Disorders that develop during adolescence.

Anxiety disorders: Disorders involving intense fear, anxiety, or worry leading to behavior directed toward avoiding or reducing the anxiety (phobias, panic disorder, obsessive-compulsive disorder, posttraumatic stress disorder).

Assessment: Observing and collecting information about the client generally during the first stages of the counseling process, but may occur throughout the counseling relationship.

Autonomous: A person who is independent or self-directed.

Behavioral: The way one behaves or acts in response to others or events.

Change: A shift in external conditions such as a new boss, a promotion, a new home, etc.

Childhood disorders: Disorders that develop during the early years of life (learning disorders, attention deficit hyperactivity disorder, tic disorders, autism).

Client: The individual seeking help from a minister for emotional difficulties, relationship issues, crisis situations, adjustment issues, and mental health issues. A client comes to a minister specifically seeking help with an identified "problem" with the expectation that the minister has the professional skills to provide assistance.

Cognitive: The way one thinks or processes information.

Cognitive disorders: Disorders involving problems in thinking that are caused by substances or medical conditions (dementia, alzheimer's, amnesia).

Competence: The development of the skills and knowledge to provide effective counseling interventions that will help clients learn to function more effectively and to utilize their talents and abilities in God's kingdom.

Conceptualization: To interpret what the client reports and what a minister observes to develop a concept of what issues are creating dysfunction in the individual's life.

Constructive thinking: Thinking patterns the clients use to help consider positive ways to change their reactions to situations and stressors.

Coping skills: Behaviors of the client that help the client deal with the current situations.

Counseling: A helping relationship whose purpose is to help an individual deal with an emotional difficulty, a relationship issue, a crisis situation, an adjustment issue, or a mental health issue.

Decompensation: The inability to respond to stress resulting in personality disturbance or psychological imbalance.

Depersonalization: Losing a normal sense of personal identity and reality.

Developmental crisis: An event in the normal flow of human life that causes a dramatic change that produces abnormal responses (birth of a child, graduating from college, career changes, retirement).

Dissociative disorders: Disorders involving an interruption in conscious awareness, memory, or identity (amnesia, fugue, dissociative identity disorder).

Distress: The experience of physical or emotional pain that may become so great that a person has difficulty functioning.

Eating disorders: Disorders involving problems in eating behaviors (anorexia, bulimia).

Educational instruction: A minister provides spiritual information in formal settings like sermons, Bible classes, and Bible lessons to individuals who are interested in learning.

Emotional: The way a person expresses feelings or processes emotional reactions.

Emotional presence: The ability to be present and in the moment for others and experience their joy and pain no matter how difficult it is.

Environmental crisis: Crisis occurring when some natural or human-caused disaster strikes a person or group of people and may affect virtually every member of the environment (hurricanes, volcanic eruptions, tornadoes, forest fires).

Existential crisis: Crisis occurring as the result of inner conflicts and anxieties related to issues of purpose, responsibility, independence, freedom, and commitment.

Factitious disorders: Conditions involving intentionally produced physical or psychological symptoms to play a sick role.

Gender identity disorders: Disorders involving problems in the normal expression of gender identity.

Genuineness: A willingness to honestly feel and express emotions toward the client and his or her life situations.

Good will: A sincere interest in the welfare of others that is not related to meeting any personal emotional needs through the counseling relationship.

Growth orientation: A commitment to investing in yourself and others to change and mold yourself to become more reflective of Christ through an appreciation for the gift of the time God has given you in this life and a willingness to try to use every moment to impact his kingdom.

Idiosyncrasy: A unique or one-of-a kind situation or reaction.

Immediate goals: Address the imminent crisis or problems that must be addressed quickly for the emotional and physical safety of the client, generally must be addressed during the session or within 24 hours.

Impairment: A reduction of a person's ability to cope and perform daily tasks.

Impulse-control disorder: Disorders involving repetition of impulsive behaviors that cause harm to self or others (kleptomania, pyromania, pathological gambling, intermittent explosive disorder).

Intervention: Counselor involvement or actions that initiate growth or change in the life of the client.

Interviewing: A minister meets with an individual once or twice to help identify the source of an emotional problem or spiritual challenge and decide what course of action to take. The client understands that a referral to someone else for assistance may be necessary if the issue cannot be addressed through spiritual teaching or mentoring.

Long-term goals: Goals addressing deeply rooted personality issues and relationship dysfunction which may take from several months to several years to change.

Listening: Requires the counselor to suspend preconceptions about clients and pay close attention to verbal and nonverbal communication so that they can present an accurate picture of who they really are.

Maladaptive: Engaging in behaviors that are not functional or do not move the individual toward adequately getting his or her needs met.

Modeling: A willingness to serve as a model for your clients and demonstrate a recognition of when you are exhibiting healthy versus unhealthy behaviors.

Mood disorders: Disorders involving emotions (depression, postpartum depression, bipolar disorder, mania).

Personal counseling style: A counseling style that is an extension and expression of your own personality and your own God-given talents.

Personal power: Recognizing one's own strength and vitality without a need to diminish others or feel superior to them.

Placating: Giving in to the demands of someone to avoid dealing with confrontation or a negative situation.

Pragmatism: A practical and matter-of-fact way of approaching counseling situations and of solving client problems.

Promotion of client self-responsibility: A commitment to helping clients trust God during the most stressful moments in their lives and become more self-reliant in problem solving.

Psychotic disorders: Disorders involving distortions in perceptions of reality (schizophrenia, delusional disorder).

Reciprocity: Occurs when both people in a relationship get some of their needs met and share their personal experiences and history with one another.

Respect: Entails a feeling of appreciation for the uniqueness of each client manifested through allowing clients to express opinions and reactions that may not be similar to your own.

Risk taking: A willingness to risk making mistakes and to admit having made them.

Risk to self or others: A danger or threat to the well-being of a person including physical or psychological welfare.

Self-worth: Recognizing and appreciating the gifts God has blessed you with.

Sexual disorders: Disorders involving problems in the normal expression of sexuality.

Short-term goals: Goals addressing changes in the client's behavior, thinking, or emotion which should occur within six to eight sessions.

Situational crisis: The occurrence of an uncommon or extraordinary event that an individual cannot control or forecast (terrorist attacks, automobile accidents, kidnappings, rapes, sudden illness or death).

Sleep disorders: Disorders involving problems in sleep behavior (insomnia, hypersomnia, nightmare disorder, sleepwalking disorder).

Somatoform disorders: Disorders involving recurring complaints of physical or medical symptoms without evidence of a medical condition (pain disorder, hypochondriasis, conversion disorder, body dysmorphic disorder).

Spiritual mentoring: A minister uses prayer, confession, Scripture reading, community service, and a personal relationship in a one-to-one or small group setting to help people strengthen their relationships with God.

Stages of counseling: The process and progression that occurs in a counseling relationship including assessment, goal setting, intervention, and evaluation of the intervention.

Substance-related disorders: Disorders related to the use or abuse of legal or illegal substances.

Support systems: People in the client's life, in the present or the past, who are concerned about the client and care what happens in the client's life.

Therapeutic progress: Progress in a counseling relationship occurs when clients become better at helping themselves and at recognizing opportunities and ways to more effectively utilize their God-given talents and abilities in the service of God's kingdom.

Transition: An emotional and cognitive reaction to change.

Trustworthiness: The trait of deserving trust and confidence by being reliable in the eyes of the client so the client can depend on your being nonjudgmental in your responses.

Vulnerability: A willingness to be open to establishing relationships and being transparent in those relationships.

About the Author

Dr. Beth Robinson is currently a Professor of Psychology and Chair of the Department of Behavioral Sciences at Lubbock Christian University in Texas. Dr. Robinson is a Licensed Professional Counselor, an Approved Supervisor for Licensed Professional Counselors, a Certified Juvenile Sex Offender Counselor, and a Certified School Counselor.

Since 1992, Dr. Robinson has worked in a variety of counseling positions. She currently has a private practice specializing in working with traumatized children and adolescents. She has previously worked as a counselor for Children's Home of Lubbock and the Panhandle Assessment Center in Amarillo, Texas; and Director of Counseling Ministries for Monterey Church of Christ in Lubbock, Texas.

In addition to her work as a counselor, she has helped prepare professionals to work in the counseling field. She has taught counselors in graduate classes at Texas Tech University and Harding University, and ministers in graduate classes at Lubbock Christian University.

Dr. Robinson earned a B.S.E. in Physical Education from Oklahoma Christian College, a M.Ed. in Educational Counseling from West Texas State University, and an Ed.D. in Counselor Education from Texas Tech University.

She has written numerous articles for publication in *Counseling and Values*, *Journal of Multicultural Counseling and Development*, *International Journal for the Advancement of Counseling*, *Guidance and Counseling*, *The Journal of Humanistic Education and Development*, and *The Journal of Theology and Psychology*. She has authored two other books: *Pass The Peanut Butter and Jelly: Inspirational Stories for Sandwiched Families* and *Sex: Helping Church Teens Deal with Challenging Issues*. Along with L.J. Bradley and E. Jarchow, she authored the book by Corwin Press, *All about Sex: The School Counselor's Guide to Handling Tough Adolescent Problems*.

Dr. Robinson is in constant demand as a speaker and trainer in universities and churches across the country. In addition, she frequently serves as a consultant to congregations on issues related to counseling. She has been active in both church ministry involvement and community service.